Center for International Affairs
Center for Middle Eastern Studies

Entrepreneurs *of* Lebanon

Entrepreneurs *of* Lebanon

The Role of the Business Leader in a Developing Economy

By Yusif A. Sayigh

Harvard University Press
1962 — Cambridge, Massachusetts

Distributed in Great Britain by Oxford University Press, London

Publication of this book has been aided by a grant from the Ford Foundation

Library of Congress Catalog Card Number 62-11404

Printed in the United States of America

AUTHOR'S PREFACE

This is a study of entrepreneurship in relation to development, applied to one country, Lebanon.

The first step undertaken has been to sketch, in Chapter 1, those realities of Lebanese conditions and life that are of direct relevance. The next step, to which Chapter 2 is devoted, is to define the context of development and to postulate the manner in which the entrepreneurial function can serve the goal of development. I have tackled the concept of entrepreneurship by suggesting the definitions and other analytical tools I consider appropriate for the circumstances of an underdeveloped, but developing, country like Lebanon. The design, method, and conduct of the study are described in Chapter 3. The conceptual framework constructed in Chapter 2 is examined in Chapter 4 against the empirical material collected for the purpose of the inquiry. It is here also that the more significant findings are reported. Finally, the broad generalizations emerging from the analysis appear in Chapter 5.

It will soon be clear that this study is both theoretical and historical. It attempts a theoretical formulation of entrepreneurship appropriate to the circumstances of underdeveloped countries, and it examines the recent experience of the entrepreneurial resources of Lebanon against this formulation. That the examination is limited to one country may be compensated for by the fact that this is probably the only investigation of such wide coverage for any country.

This study was made possible through a generous grant by the Rockefeller Foundation, thanks to the special interest of the late Norman S. Buchanan who was then Director of the Social Sciences. This grant enabled the Economic Research Institute at the American University of Beirut, on whose faculty I serve, to allow me the time needed for research between 1957 and 1959.

The writing of the book was undertaken at Harvard University during the year 1959–60, under a joint research grant by the Center for Middle Eastern Studies and the Center for International Affairs. I am grateful to Professors H. A. R. Gibb, Robert R. Bowie, and A. J. Meyer, of the two centers, for the opportunity they afforded me to devote the time to write the manuscript in an intellectually stimulating atmosphere. Professor Meyer was all along a source of help and encouragement.

Support, guidance, and valuable criticism came through all stages from Dr. Fritz Redlich, who also read the first draft of the manuscript. Professors Edward S. Mason, Everett E. Hagen, A. J. Meyer, and Lleland Jenks also kindly read the manuscript and gave me the benefit of their observations and comments. I owe special thanks to Professor Mason for writing an introduction to the book.

I would like also to acknowledge my appreciation of the efficient help I received from the team of research assistants in Beirut who did most of the interviewing, all of the coding of the questionnaires used for the study, and the preparation and checking of the hundreds of tables in which the data were recorded. They are: Miss Dolly Hakim, Miss Soraya Antonius, Miss Madge Saleeby, Mr. Sami Baaklini, Dr. Bashir Daouk, Mr. Elias Saba, Mr. Ramzi Malouf, and Mr. Yahya Mahmassani. Miss Wadad Abboud and Miss Lamia Awad handled the statistical machines under the direction of Mr. Baaklini.

Having acknowledged my debt to the many institutions and persons who contributed to the conduct of this study, I hasten to add that all blame for the shortcomings of the book rests on me alone.

Y. A. S.

CONTENTS

TABLES

INTRODUCTION

The part of the world that is now Lebanon has, from the beginning of recorded time, never lacked for businessmen. From the days of the Phoenicians to the present, the denizens of the Levant have, in extraordinary numbers, made their living by buying and selling, exchanging monies, exporting and importing, serving as middlemen at all stages from the first production to the final disposition of products. Their activities have carried them throughout the Middle East, around the Mediterranean, down the east and west coasts of Africa, across Asia and, in latter times, to such outlandish outposts as São Paulo and Detroit.

Nor, until very recent times, has the characteristic activity of the typical Lebanese businessman changed very much. Lebanon presents the odd example of an economy two thirds of whose income is generated in the service area. The total net value of the products of agriculture, manufacturing, mining, and construction accounts for only one third of national income. Those who see economic development as a movement from primary (agricultural), to secondary (industrial), to tertiary (service) activity might be forced to conclude that Lebanon is already the most developed country in the world with very little, if any, place to go.

Indeed, by Middle Eastern standards, Lebanon is a highly developed country. Apart from a few oil-rich sheikdoms, it has the highest per capita income in the Arab world, and other indices of economic well-being tell the same story. But $350 per capita per annum, though high for the Middle East, is not quite affluence. Moreover, the trading, banking, and exchange activities that have brought Lebanon to its present position seem destined to rather severe limitation through political and economic changes in the surrounding Arab world. Lebanon's future development may require structural and cultural changes that will make it somewhat less of a trading community than it has been at times in the remote and recent past.

Dr. Sayigh is concerned with this development, which he conceives as a social process inadequately described by national income statistics. He is especially concerned with the role of the entrepreneur in the process. For his purpose it is not sufficient to identify entrepreneur with businessman, particularly not with the businessman-as-trader so typical of the Lebanese scene. He borrows from Schumpeter the conception of entrepreneur as innovator, the initiator of new combinations of resources, or the introducer of new products to new markets. But in borrowing, Dr. Sayigh adapts. It is enough for him that the entrepreneur proceed not *de novo,* but as a man who takes from elsewhere and shapes what he takes to suit the local scene. The entrepreneur must, however, introduce something new to the Lebanese economy to merit the title and to justify a prime role as an agent of economic development. Who are these people, where do they come from, how are they shaped by, and how do they shape, their environment?

The environment is in many ways ideal for the cultivation of this kind of talent which has, in fact, emerged in substantial numbers since the last war. The Lebanese encircle the world; their trading activities and travels bring them in touch continuously with products and processes that have possibilities of adaptation to Lebanese production and use. The trading mentality, it is true, is not necessarily easy to convert to other types of economic activity, nor are the educational practices and cultural environment well adapted to the generation of other than trading pursuits. Not many businessmen have the competence or desire to become entrepreneurs, as Dr. Sayigh uses the term, but there have been enough to merit study.

Not only do Lebanese businessmen have the contacts and connections necessary to the process of borrowing and adapting techniques and commodities, but also the domestic environment is peculiarly suited to money-making. In many ways, the economic environment is mid-nineteenth century; it is Manchester in its most pristine form. Taxes are low and apparently rather easily evaded; government regulation is lax; tariffs are rather low and there are no foreign exchange controls. If little government means good government, the government of Lebanon must be one of the best. In fact, of course, a relatively inefficient and corrupt government is hardly an unmixed blessing for private enterprise, and though the scale of tariff duties is highly favorable to the trading community it is not universally admired in the nascent industrial sector.

The economic impetus to development in this situation has come, and will clearly continue to come, from the private sector. This in itself distinguishes Lebanon from most of the underdeveloped world. Developing countries in Asia and the rest of the Middle East tend to rely heavily on public initiative to start into motion the wheels of expansion. Not only does the share of the public sector in total capital formation tend to be large, but governments shape, through exchange controls, licensing, price regulation, and other means, the direction and character of private investment. In Lebanon, on the other hand, entrepreneurial endeavor unimpeded and undirected by government is the principal economic agent of change.

It is difficult, considering the political structure of the country, to envision how it could be otherwise. Lebanon is a curious mixture of "political feudalism" and a rather extreme version of nineteenth-century economic liberalism. Politics splits along confessional lines, and the relative position of the various confessors is formally recognized in the constitution. Members of the various faiths tend to vote as directed by their leaders, and the method of appointment to public office frustrates the emergence of a civil service based on merit. The result is a government capable, in ordinary times, of maintaining law and order and of providing a minimum structure of public services, but of not much else. Certainly it is not capable of taking active leadership in the development process.

This does not mean, however, that development will not take place. The private sector is as active as the public is supine. Putting the trading sector aside, Dr. Sayigh has examined the phenomenon of entrepreneurship in the fields of manufacture, agriculture, banking, and certain of the service industries. Starting with some 8000 firms, he has narrowed the number down to some 207 that meet both the tests of his definitions of entrepreneurship and of availability of data. Of these, well over half, 130, were in the manufacturing area. Dr. Sayigh considers the national and denominational affiliations of the innovating decision-makers in the 207 firms, their social and cultural background, and their training, education, and experience outside of business. As one might expect, he feels this to be an untypical group of Lebanese businessmen; it is, after all, a group selected on the basis of demonstrated capacity to innovate.

Finally, Dr. Sayigh considers the contribution of entrepreneurship to economic development in Lebanon, and the practical question of how public policies might accelerate the flow of entrepreneurial talent. Although Lebanon is a small country and, for reasons given above, not very typical of much of the underdeveloped world, these are critical questions to be faced in any country seeking to move forward toward a process of self-sustaining growth.

Edward S. Mason
Center for International Affairs
Harvard University

Entrepreneurs *of* Lebanon

Chapter I

THE ENVIRONMENT

THE small Lebanese population, which numbers about one million and a half, is the most literate and sophisticated of Arab peoples.[1] And the most fragmented. The mountainous terrain has always acted as an asylum for religious minorities and other groups in search of freedom from oppression; there is, therefore, a large number of splinter denominations of Christianity and Islam, in addition to the orthodox denominations living mainly in the coastal towns.

Denominational separateness is still evident. The Ottoman "Millet" system, according to which the personal affairs of the various non-Moslem communities were ruled by their own religious jurisdictions and courts, has helped to keep these communities divided among themselves and separated from the Moslem communities. The superiority of denominational schools (which until recently have had widely divergent curricula) over the national school system has retarded thorough fusion. The fanning of divisive forces, from time to time, by internal as well as external interested parties has been an added reason for continued fragmentation. The cumulative influence of all these factors shows itself in the social and political, as well as the economic spheres of life.

Thus, although socially there is very little class differentation between landowner, townsman-merchant, or manual laborer, and relations across class lines are unhindered, sectarianism has turned the communities into separate groups vying with each other *as groups* for power and benefits. This is not merely a pattern established by custom and convention but one formalized through the incorporation of its principle in the Constitution.[2] The importance and power of the clergy in such a social structure are obvious, and clergymen have not been slow to realize this and turn it to advantage.

Two serious problems related to sectarianism weigh heavily on the wheels of social and economic progress. The first is "political feudalism" which characterizes a system of political relationships between share tenants and large landowners in the plains area, between small estate owners and descendants of the ruling elite of the past two or three centuries in the mountain area, and between the city mass (mostly immigrants from the countryside) and influential politicians whose power largely derives from origins in the countryside supplemented by urban political affiliations and economic affluence. The followers in this system owe allegiance to the leader personally and support him in elections. On the leader's side, the obligation is to seek benefits and public works funds for his men, help them out if they fall into trouble, and generally act as their political guardian.

Luckily this anomalous feature of the electoral system is giving way to a truer expression of the electorate's will. However, a second problem exists, even more closely related to sectarianism. This is "political confessionalism" whereby parliamentary seats are allotted according to an agreed pattern to the various religious communities.[3] The general recognition of their assumed rights leads the communities to consider that the best safeguard for their rights is adequate representation in parliament through people of their own religious denomination. The sectarian pattern is not restricted to the seats of parliament. By precedent, it governs the distribution of executive offices, from that of the president of the republic down to the level of section chief in a ministry.

The combined effect of political feudalism and political confessionalism has been to push the unqualified man forward if he is of the right sect and has the necessary backing; to produce inefficiency and superfluity in the civil service; and to give the laws of the land little authority and effectiveness — in short, to retard far-reaching reform in all aspects of society's life. Although the public at large is aware of the necessity of reform, it is generally kept so busy with its community rivalries that it leaves the field virtually free for narrow vested interests.

The system of education is in fact many private and public systems. It has produced a relatively high level of literacy, though of doubtful immediate value for purposes of fast economic growth. The emphasis has all along been on liberal arts and law, to the detriment of the scientific, the technical, and the vocational. A high premium is placed on mental "cleverness," on verbal prowess, which is not the best preparation for facing a country's material problems. This is more pertinently so the greater the urgency for a shift in the structure of the Lebanese economy away from trade and services toward commodity production. As a result of this urgency a shift in the content of curricula has begun to take place. But the supply of scientists, engineers, and economists remains much less adequate than that of lawyers and poets.

However, the influence of their one-sided education has not made the Lebanese much less resourceful, less shrewd, or less adventurous. The heritage of the Phoenicians is in demonstrable abundance. The Lebanese keep their eyes on the far seas for better economic opportunities. Prompted by ambition as well as the paucity of resources and the hardships of life (and in older times by the insecurity culminating in the denominational strife of 1860), hundreds of thousands of Lebanese have emigrated to the Americas, Australia and New Zealand, Africa, and recently to the Arab oil region. Apart from long-established contacts with the West provided by trade, foreign missions, and schools, and by military occupation, emigration has forged strong ties with the outside world and has been of great influence in the transmission of ideas, new methods, and new forms of organization, as well as of remittances.[4]

The Phoenician heritage of adventure, trade, and brisk business enterprise has been supplemented by attitudes attributable to Arab temperament, such as versatility and impatience. Thus here again, as in many other respects, Lebanese society shows the strains and stresses of mixed parentage.

Given social fragmentation, there will clearly be limited cohesiveness within the groups of which the society is composed but looseness where relations between groups are concerned. Under such conditions, the Lebanese businessman emerges as a die-hard individualist, and individualism leads him toward economic sectors and activities, such as trade and services, where individual operation or operation in small partnerships commends itself most. Furthermore, fragmentation and competitiveness between the groups in the political field of necessity produce entrepreneurial resilience and intense drive in economic pursuits. Material success probably compensates for the frustrations and limitations to personal ambition set by the rigidity of social-cultural-political groupings.

Certain common features of the local culture underlie as well as reflect the results of individualism and competitiveness, for example, the traditional prestige which generally attaches to commerce and foreign trade, the accumulation of proverbs and sayings playing up the superiority of business ventures singly operated, the pride taken in adventurousness as exemplified in willingness to emigrate in search of opportunity, the love of freedom and independence, and the restlessness and the pace of life generally. The religious beliefs to which the three major communities of Christians, Moslems, and Druses subscribe do not seem to produce a conclusive effect on economic drive and motivation, either of a promotive or of an inhibitive nature. The Lebanese *homo oeconomicus* seems more to reflect the influence of other elements in his cultural heritage than religious doctrine.

The individualism, competitiveness, and agility which characterize the actors in the Lebanese economy operate in an atmosphere of extreme freedom. This freedom is many-sided. The country has liberal trade policies (in spite of the pressure of the emerging industrial interests for restrictions), a minimally controlled banking system, a completely uncontrolled foreign exchange market, and an almost unchallenged free-enterprise sector. This sector is large and free both because private entrepreneurs are set on keeping it to themselves, and because the government has no urge to encroach.

The freedom has incongruous roots. It is partly the result of an innate revolt against control and regulation and a genuine love of freedom. But it is also the result of a serious moral-political crisis in Lebanese society. For it has been the sad experience of this society that an unduly high proportion of politicians and executives have since independence in 1946 been only too well aware of the ease with which the spoils of office can accrue to the unscrupulous. They have likewise been aware of the safety with which these spoils can be snatched away when the public is in a general mood of cynical resignation. Temptation and its fulfillment are curbed neither by moral considerations nor by society's sanctions. The guilty almost invariably in time enjoy absolution from the good-natured public; they even enjoy the esteem of hopeful emulators. This anomalous situation is further confounded, in the context of the social mosaic, by the hesitation of any one group (assuming it possessed greater political morality than the others) to press hard for reform, or even to practice this morality alone. Frustrated, the scrupulous find that they are the losers, that they are neither "smart" nor effective. The corrupt naturally do not want corrective action by government; the honest are largely unable to bring about reform; both think government action unlikely.

The population displays a dual reaction to this situation. The enterprising go on with their plans and projects, relying on themselves, and score successes in many fields. Indeed, some of the strength of the private sector in the economy may result from the fact that it has had to survive and flourish notwithstanding the paucity of assistance from the public sector. (This is not to say, however, that the private sector would not have developed further and faster had the political and administrative machine been more efficient and its personnel more honest.[5]) The less enterprising, although they do not have much confidence in the government, do not tire of asking it to do things they think it unlikely or unable to do. So long as the paradoxical attitude of the less enterprising continues, the level of the government's achievement cannot match the level of expectation by the public. In such an atmosphere, the state's agencies will not be forced to take a more responsible and effective role.

In the midst of the social and political setting we have sketched there is, by and large, a marked degree of political security and stability, a stability based upon the countervailing forces of the fragmented society. Supplemented by the innate adventurousness and optimism of the Lebanese, the stability creates a climate that encourages economic drive and promotes enterprise despite political limitations imposed by the precariousness of external political relations and the lack of regional cooperation. The limitations tend to sharpen the resourcefulness and resilience of Lebanese enterprise; only in extreme cases do they inhibit enterprise or limit growth in scale of operations and expansion abroad.

A few shortcomings of the institutional framework must be mentioned for their influence on the emergence of innovational enterprise and on the pace of growth. Only in the last few years has credit for industrial and agricultural investment begun to be available at low cost in relatively adequate volume.[6] Research facilities are limited and the readiness to use them is not very wide: indeed, there is little evident belief in the practical value of research for the business community.

Business legislation has not developed as fast as economic activity, and the new relationships characteristic of a developing economy now require radical accommodation by the body of business legislation. The most striking lag is that of corporate organization behind the conditions that make the corporation an appropriate form of business association. This gap is partly the result of the individualist temperament prevailing, but also partly the result of a legacy of outmoded legislation originating in the days of the French mandate. The country also lacks the appropriate legal framework for the promotion of good standards in the fields of marketing, advertising, product specification, accounting, and auditing.

On the credit side of the picture is a good road system, adequate transport facilities, and a light tax burden. In addition to the low rates of the income tax, evasion seems to be easy for the ingenious. Furthermore, new manufacturing corporations satisfying certain conditions (including novelty of product manufactured) are exempt from corporate tax for six years after establishment. This concession has proved attractive to the enterprising and has had some value in promoting corporate organization.

In the broader area of technology the picture is even brighter. Here the Lebanese display both the readiness and the ability to learn new methods. This statement may sound surprising in view of the quality and directions of education described earlier. But it is in agreement with the Lebanese traits of resilience and resourcefulness reinforced by the intensity of the drive for material success, by the fierceness of competition, and by the quickness of pace of economic life generally. With the new shift in the content of curricula away from liberal arts and law toward science, engineering, and economics and business administration, the combination of education and personality with motivational traits will very likely produce a quicker pace of technological change capable of sustaining and even intensifying the process of development.

This, then, is the broad setting within which the economic actors operate. The product displays all the peculiarities of the setting. The over-all performance of the economy is very good by Afro-Asian standards. After a spell of continuous growth since the war, national income currently averages about $325 per capita. The services-producing sectors (trade, finance, transport, resorts, government, and other services) contribute some two thirds of the national income as against one third by the commodity-producing sectors (agriculture, mining, construction, and manufacturing)[7] — an unusual ratio indeed.

The economic and social structure underlying the ratio and the forces and factors shaping the structure have been the subject of examination by serious-minded observers, but more often of speculation by mystics and obscurantists.[8] In fact, both the structure and the ratio it produces are quite understandable given the social and political setting and the circumstances of the country. Fitting into the center of the Asian front on the Mediterranean, Lebanon is within convenient reach of suppliers and markets, and therefore enjoys a suitable location for trade and transit services. (These activities alone account for over one fourth of national income.) Means of transportation have certainly changed, but the modern Lebanese trader and middleman, no less than his Phoenician and Arab ancestors, takes full advantage of his country's location and of his own skill to collect wares from suppliers and spread them in markets far and wide. The pressure of poverty in natural resources reinforces the advantages of location, temperament, and tradition.

The financial sector has developed considerably to service the flourishing import-export and transit trade. In recent years this sector has attracted, and benefited from, a flow of deposits coming from the oil-rich centers of the Arab world.[9] Capital funds have therefore been quite adequate for local short-term requirements. This advantage is strengthened by the monetary stability of the country. The Lebanese pound has kept its parity with the U.S. dollar for several years now.[10] Furthermore, foreign exchange resources are quite plentiful. No importer who has available the pound equivalent has difficulty in finding foreign exchange — whether it is U.S. dollars, Swiss francs, or Chinese yen.

The location and the scenic beauty of the country, and the appealing taste of its artisans, have combined to promote tourism and personal services by attracting thousands upon thousands of foreign visitors who come to enjoy what the country has to offer by way of climate, entertainment, clothing, and good drink and food.

Other services that are important earners of foreign exchange are schools and hospitals, and contracting. The contractor, perhaps more than the trader, is today the roving emissary of Lebanon. Contractors have been quick to seize the opportunities arising in the oil region in the Middle East from the vast expenditures made on public works (roads, bridges, schools, oil installations, housing schemes) and private building (ranging from modest villas to princely palaces).

However, serious consequences derive from the occupation by trade and services of the place of honor in the economy. They are of an economic and a noneconomic nature.

It is true that the prosperity of trade and services reflects a brisk and refined business sense, sensitivity to world markets and to price fluctuations, mental alertness, skill in trading and in the performance of services, and an ability to cater to clients' tastes. But the Lebanese tend to take undue pride in the fact that theirs is a services economy, and consequently neither industry nor agriculture receives the attention it deserves from government, or the esteem it deserves from the rest of the business community. The industrial sector has grown rapidly since the war, both in relative importance as a contributor to the national income and in quality and diversification of products. Agriculture lies between trade and industry in the ranking of sectors on the basis of their contribution to the national income. The strong point of Lebanese agriculture is the excellence of its vegetables and fruits. Lebanese fruits, because of their high quality, have been successful in many European markets, Western and Eastern, despite the exporters' failure to develop effective grading, packing, and marketing mechanisms and practices, and to respect shipment specifications rigorously.

The favors that merchants enjoy and the power they wield in policy-making draw the opposition of the industrialists. Industrial interests are at variance with trade interests over trade policy, credit policy, and the role of the state in promoting economic development. Industrialists insist on more restrictive tariffs, more and longer-term credit facilities for investment, and milder laisser faire convictions.

Several factors indicate that the merchant class will lose its dominant position. There is first the growth of the industrial sector and the gain in strength by industrialists that is bound to follow. Second, there is the stiffening opposition that the Lebanese trading middleman is meeting in Syria, Jordan, Iraq, and other areas in the region, where his services are now at best barely tolerated and at worst forbidden. Importers and wholesalers generally in these places want to develop skill in foreign trade and to establish contact with their foreign suppliers and clients directly, instead of through the traditional intermediary of the Lebanese. Serious effort is being made to divert trade from the Beirut port to Latakia in Syria, Aqaba in Jordan, and Basrah in Iraq. On the other hand, Lebanese industrialists wishing to participate with Syrian, Jordanian, or Iraqi industrialists in new ventures, or even to set up their own factories, are still welcome to do so subject to certain reasonable limitations.

And third, the merger of Syria and Egypt in 1958 into the United Arab Republic led to the gradual integration of the two economies and intensified the trend, already manifest before 1958, toward the dissociation of the Syrian from the Lebanese economy. The seriousness of this trend for Lebanese trade arises from the fact that Syria used to be the best customer of Lebanon even after the two ceased to form an economic union in March 1950. (In the early fifties Lebanese exports to Syria were just under half its total exports. Today they are less than one third.) The dissolution of the union between Syria and Egypt is too recent for its effects on the Lebanese economy to be evaluated. However, even if Syria decides to pursue a liberal economic policy, it will probably not allow Lebanese businessmen the freedom of enterprise in its territory which they enjoyed until the early fifties, any more than it did when it was part of the United Arab Republic.

The bias in favor of services in Lebanese society raises misgivings not only because of the subordination of agriculture and industry. In this trade-centered society, cleverness enjoys a premium over creativity. The emphasis on gains made through clever bargaining is greater than the emphasis on steady business relations and on deals based on the respective merits of the goods exchanged. And the search for a quick turnover and large easy profits accentuates an inclination to speculative enterprise and militates against sustained effort and long-term investment promising long-term, though low, profit rates. "Catering," which is a major feature in a services-biased economy, is an attitude and a frame of mind. Its imprint on the quality of entrepreneurial resources and on entrepreneurial behavior can hardly be escaped.

Chapter 2

IN SEARCH OF ENTREPRENEURS

THE quest for entrepreneurs in any country can be justified on two grounds. The first is the importance of their role, as a group, in the promotion of economic growth and the enrichment of its quality. The second is the importance of their position between the broad environment within which they operate, on the one hand, and the individual firms for and on behalf of which they operate, on the other hand.* Entrepreneurs, of course, assume special significance in the kind of economic and social system assumed here — one in which most of the means of production are in private hands and are allocated according to decentralized decisions by profit-seeking firms.[1] One's conception of the role and position of the entrepreneurs in such a system depends in large measure on one's understanding of the content of development.

THE CONTENT OF DEVELOPMENT

A striking characteristic of many underdeveloped regions of the world today is that they are struggling to go through several revolutions simultaneously. Side by side, though at varying stages of their

* In the empirical portions of this book the term "establishment" will be used instead of "firm" because of the stronger appeal of the former as a clear operational term.

unfolding, emerge the political, the socio-economic, and the technological revolutions which in Western Europe spanned several centuries. What for the West is already history, is for the underdeveloped world still current experience.

The upheaval brought about by the revolutions is manifest in all aspects of life. At its root is the burning desire to achieve progress, no matter how variously defined, on numerous fronts. It seeks victory over outside conquerors and victory over the two major internal evils: physical need and social degradation.

The brisk pace at which change is permeating the old order is very exacting for underdeveloped countries. Economic change, being the vehicle for a fundamental and restless striving in the political and cultural realms, acquires great significance. This is especially true of the ex-colonial areas which, after long years of foreign domination, are only now experiencing the exhilarating excitement of national statehood—an experience which even for the New World is already old. Strongly aware of the time lag, they act under great pressure.

The underdeveloped countries face serious challenges. There is, first, the challenge created mainly from within through the society's realization of its economic and social backwardness and its desire to narrow the gap between itself and some other society which it views as a model. A second challenge comes from without. Contact with the West and the rival Communist world has accentuated the urge of the internal challenge. Response to the internal and external challenges in all but the most backward societies inevitably leads to action, and places before the underdeveloped society a third challenge: one arising from the dynamics of social action. For, in accepting the challenges from within and from without, the underdeveloped country has consciously to make, and to continue making, numberless decisions at all levels of responsibility and in all fields, from whose disruptive and transformative effects no aspect of life remains immune. And it is precisely the consciousness of the urgency of decision-making, the decisions made, the actions taken to embody the decisions, and the chain of effects following the actions, which inject dynamism into otherwise stagnant or slowly changing societies.

This picture of the response to challenge obviously portrays an idealized process. Between the present, when the process may be nebulous, and the future, when it can unfold more fully, lies a long course of social and economic action loaded with complex problems. But the one over-all problem which confronts underdeveloped countries generally is the meeting of the insistent challenges created by their social, economic, and scientific and technical backwardness, *in spite* of the backwardness itself. This is the impasse in the course of progress which most underdeveloped countries are struggling to break through. In my opinion, the breakthrough itself signifies development.

In this sense, development is a process as well as a state, since the breakthrough, while signifying a society's success in overcoming many of its economic and noneconomic problems and its transformation into a more developed state, is also a continuing act of change through time. Furthermore, in the sense in which the terms are used here, development is something beyond growth: it is growth of a certain order and on certain conditions.

Along this line of thought, it is useful to consider underdevelopment and development together, both as parts of one process and as stages in one model of economic progress. Indeed, the classification of countries as developed or underdeveloped must be taken as merely an expedient convention where the particular result obtained is the inevitable offspring of the definitions and criteria of development that happen to be used.

In my view, the determining factor in making this classification should be the sudden spurt which may occur in the course of the steady rate of growth of real income in stagnant or slowly growing economies.[2] This acceleration in growth has to be sustained for a considerable time to be of significance, and during the period of accelerated growth, development should be gaining from year to year more than it had been gaining before the jump in the rate of growth, although in absolute terms the rate may still be considerably lower than that characterizing a more developed economy.

The original social setting preceding this accelerated, sustained growth has certain features common to all underdeveloped countries, in spite of minor variations. Countries broadly conforming to the model here described have a low real income per capita — something below $350 or $300 a year. This in itself reflects the low performance of the economy. Simultaneous with the low level of the national product, and functionally connected with it, is a social-political structure which is incapable of sustaining an economy that can produce a much larger national product. Furthermore, in such countries economic affluence, social position, and political power are concentrated in the hands of the few.

It follows that development, while essentially resting on the requirement of accelerated growth in real income, should be further associated with certain other requirements to be sustained beyond a critical stage. Thus:

1) The political and social environment should be able to provide the economy with many of the ideas, knowledge, attitudes, and institutions essential to efficient functioning;

2) The bulk of the material progress achieved should be the result of the performance of the community, not of large islands of foreign enterprise in the midst of a poorly performing economic organization;

3) The pattern of income distribution should at least not be one of greater polarization than before development for any considerable length of time, otherwise the bulk of the population will be deprived of the fruits of material progress; and

4) Technological and other change should continue in considerable measure, in order to enable the economy to sustain the rise in the rate of growth, or to sustain the rate itself if it has reached a high level.

Where does entrepreneurship, both as a function and as a "commonalty of entrepreneurs,"[3] fit into this broad view of development? As said earlier, entrepreneurship has an important role to play in the process of development and an important position to fill between environment and its operating economic units. Both the role and the position become clear in the context of the multisided challenge of underdevelopment and of the content of development.

The point can be stated briefly. The economic expression of the responses to the challenge, in its comprehensiveness and depth, can only come through the actions of innovating decision-makers in the economic field. And these actions can be of the right caliber only if they involve radical change in the economy, in diversification, quantitative growth, and quality improvement. None of the usual growth factors can have significant weight in the absence of enterprise. Population increase is a passive force; it is enterprise that effects the expansion necessary in response to the increase. Changes in tastes are perhaps as much induced as spontaneous, but in either case it is enterprise that effects the necessary changes in productive and distributive processes to satisfy new tastes. Advances in technology remain a mere economic potential until enterprise applies them and turns them into a motive force for development. The extension of the frontier, where it occurs, is an act of men who have new business ideas, who plan, and who act: in other words, an entrepreneurial act.

This economic response is expressed through individual economic units in action, but it involves the whole economy. If it falls short of such dimensions, it will hover on the edge of growth and will fail to qualify as development. That in itself will be an indication that changes in technology and in social and political institutions have not quite reached the point where the community's economic performance can carry it to the desired shore of development.

Failure to develop poses a grave menace to the needy populations and the precarious political and economic systems of poor, struggling societies. The search for entrepreneurs cannot, then, fail to be a matter of first importance to these societies and of immense interest to students of development.

WHAT IS AN ENTREPRENEUR?

The function, the role, and the identity of the entrepreneur have been the subject of a great deal of sophisticated discussion since the time when, in 1755, Richard Cantillon designated as "entrepreneurs" those who "buy the wares of the country . . . give for them a fixed price to sell them again wholesale and retail at an uncertain price."[4] Crude as this definition may seem, it succeeds nevertheless in bringing out the element of initiative in the entrepreneur's character, the element of mediation in his role, and the element of uncertainty in his function with all that it implies in rewards and penalties.

Economists and other social scientists have, since Cantillon, asked more and more questions about entrepreneurship. However, a review of the place of the entrepreneur in economic theory will not be attempted here, as it would carry us far afield. The immediate task is to examine entrepreneurial theory in its application to the underdeveloped world, with a view to finding the salient characteristics of the entrepreneur and the locus of enterprise, and to understanding how satisfactorily and in what fashion the entrepreneur, or the "business leader" as we shall alternatively call him in an empirical context, fulfills his role in the process of accelerated growth. (The adjectival form of the word "entrepreneur" will, however, be used, since no such form of the phrase "business leader" exists. "Entrepreneurship" and "enterprise" will also be used, interchangeably.)

That entrepreneurial theory, as it now stands, largely reflects the time and environment of its emergence is amply confirmed by the way in which the tenets of the theory accommodate the facts of the period and of the locale to which the theory applies. True enough, there have been lags in this accommodation, with theory moving slowly behind historical reality. On the other hand, there have been prophetic anticipations of the "shape of things to come," when theory moved ahead of actual development in the economic system.[5]

The Western world, which is the birthplace of the contemporary theory of enterprise and the seat of the economies to which it relates, fits the theory snugly. Thus, to talk of plural entrepreneurship in the Western large corporation, or of the entrepreneurial function of the banking system characteristic of Wall Street or the City, or of the long-range expectations of the individual business leader engaged in heavy investment in a stable developed society — to talk of any of these in the context of Karachi or Aleppo or Bogota is to use alien terms which jar with dimensions of time and place. Hence the urgency of an entrepreneurial theory in harmony with conditions in the underdeveloped country of today.

I add "today" in order to underline the significance of the coexistence, alongside underdeveloped countries, of more developed ones in possession of a more developed theory. Such coexistence will influence entrepreneurial theory for the underdeveloped country by forcing it to become flexible and open to deviation from the channels of experience which the theory for the developed country has followed.

This is not to say that there are, or there ought to be, two clearcut theories of enterprise: one relevant to the developed, and the other to the underdeveloped country. It is more reasonable to argue that entrepreneurship is a system of action that changes form as time passes; different countries will be passing through different stages in the evolution of the system at any one moment. Moreover, the gaps separating these stages are under strong pressure to become narrower. The "migration of ideas" [6] is much freer today than it has ever been, although the movement of persons and capital funds is not as free. Furthermore, social, political, and economic pressures make for a rapid narrowing of the gaps, as the present study tries to show.

The conduct of the investigation required a definition of the nature and the purpose of the search for entrepreneurs in Lebanon. Certain questions and postulates were therefore formulated as a framework for the study by the summer of 1958. This framework was to serve as a basis for the design and preparation of a questionnaire that was to be used later in the interviewing of all businessmen qualifying as entrepreneurs, and as a frame of reference in the arrangement, analysis, and appraisal of the data that were expected from the interviews. The rest of this chapter is largely a reproduction of the original formulation.

Innovational Enterprise and Its Implications

The foremost question has to do with the entrepreneurial function and the identification of the business leader. The question has been, and still is, of theoretical interest. It also has practical significance for this study, for an inquiry into the entrepreneurial resources of a country is not possible without a working definition of entrepreneurship.

No hard and fast rule can be laid down as to the type of man who can play the entrepreneurial role under the conditions and requirements of development in a predominantly private-enterprise system. The entrepreneurial function which he has to be able to fulfill comprises a number of variations: from primary or creative innovation at the top, down to the point of routine management. All aspects of the function are essential, each in its own way and its appropriate time, but only those involving innovation, at least in the sense of adoption of "new combinations" existing in other countries, are capable of leading to development. The term "new combinations" is used here in the Schumpeterian sense and applies equally to new products, new processes, new forms of organization, new markets, or new sources of supply.[7] However, these new combinations need not be sensational or dramatic as in the Schumpeterian model, but only modestly new for the locale where they are being applied.

This broad definition of "innovation" is essential. For perhaps more important than a creative or primary form of innovation introduced only infrequently and in a few isolated cases, is a much more frequent and more widely diffused introduction of derivative innovations — indeed, of mere adaptation to local conditions, and imitation of innovations generated outside the underdeveloped locale. The introduction of derivative innovations may not in any one case entail a large dose of radical change in the economy, but it produces greater change in a larger number of establishments than would be possible with primary innovation. Furthermore, derivative innovation brings closer the building up of a tradition of entrepreneurship, increases the size of entrepreneurial resources, and quickens the evolution of an entrepreneurial organization within the industry or establishment[8] and ultimately of an entrepreneurial stream or system in society as a whole.[9]

This view represents a deviation from Joseph Schumpeter's. Thus, while I emphasize innovation in the *content* of the entrepreneurial function, I subscribe neither to the conditions that Schumpeter attaches to the quality of innovation nor to the form and medium through which, according to him, the entrepreneurial function is discharged. It will be recalled that in Schumpeter's view the entrepreneur is a man who, owing to exceptional personality traits, carries through innovations of importance for the industry and the economy. It is for these innovations (involving new combinations) that Schumpeter reserves the term "enterprise." [10] Classified according to the chronology of their occurrence, the three phases of the entrepreneurial function are conception or perception of innovation; promotion of a business organization capable of embodying the innovation (considered by Schumpeter the pure form of entrepreneurship); and inception (which involves the actual putting into effect of the innovation).[11] Such a framework is too restrictive to suit the conditions of contemporary underdeveloped economies. It is reasonable to maintain, with Schumpeter, that only decision-making with regard to innovation — not decision-making in itself — is an entrepreneurial function. But it would be both unrealistic and unfruitful, in the context of a study of enterprise in an underdeveloped country, to define innovation narrowly. Consequently, the position is taken here that innovations of a derivative (adaptive) nature are indeed innovations and constitute enterprise in this type of country.[12]

As it is used in this study, the term "innovation" is only a shorthand expression for a range of decisions that business leaders must be capable of making if they are to merit the designation of leadership. These decisions fall into the fields of technology, organization, selling and markets, research, public relations, employment, coordination of productive inputs, and even management—the function which is clearly beneath the entrepreneur in Schumpeter's view. The business leader would normally make two or more of these types of decisions simultaneously, although the emphasis would shift with the change of the circumstances of the establishment.

Schumpeter's entrepreneur is an exceptional, almost solitary figure. This is true in the sense that the entrepreneur strikes out in new paths as far as his locale is concerned. But he is a more common type in the conditions of the present day, and research and planned teamwork make his contribution almost predictable. Thus, the medium of human resource through which the complex of entrepreneurial functions is discharged in our contemporary world is quite different from that postulated by Schumpeter. This base of human resource is broader owing both to the changed structure of business generally, and to diversification in the content of the function as I have defined it.

The starting point in this study is that the entrepreneur is the authority in a firm who makes decisions with regard to innovation, by way of adoption of new combinations as well as effective organization, whether the innovation requires the setting up of a new firm or is adopted in a going concern.

The entrepreneur performs a function distinct from the capital-owner, and is not necessarily the risk-bearer. However, innovation increases uncertainty within the firm (in the sense of unquantifiable, therefore conventionally uninsurable, risk), and the entrepreneur will ordinarily be concerned with adequate provision for this uncertainty. The non-capital-owning business leader (including the manager who performs an entrepreneurial function) is directly affected by economic profit (positive or negative) which results from the application of new combinations or from reorganization.

The ultimate beneficiary of the profit is the capital-owner or the labor force, or both, depending on the relative power of the two groups; but to the extent that part of profits goes to management in the form of commissions, bonuses, or higher salaries, and to the extent that profit carries with it security (whether of position or of financial reward) the manager is also a beneficiary.[13]

The qualification ought to be added that the adoption of uncertainty-increasing combinations or of reorganization by the business leader has to have the continuity and success of the firm as an objective, however "success" is defined by him. Decisions involving an unjustifiably high degree of uncertainty — a degree at which the very being of the firm is endangered — defeat the purpose of the firm. Thus, although the business leader is the man who is empowered to make decisions that may be suicidal as far as his existence as businessman is concerned, we are interested only in those decisions which in the first place enable an entrepreneurial idea to be embodied in a firm, and in the second place — once the firm is established or reorganized as a result — aid it to continue and grow.[14]

For the purposes of this study, and indeed in conformity with my definition and understanding of entrepreneurship, the entrepreneur need not necessarily be a "businessman" strictly speaking. He may also be a scientist or technician, a salesman, an organizer, or a public relations man — in other words, any man who has power of decision in or for an enterprise. But we do not expect him to be all of these combined. Any of these men, if so empowered, may make decisions regarding combinations of such a significance for the firm that they may be termed entrepreneurial. It may be useful to find out to what extent, if any, the locus of enterprise shifts from the capital-owner as such to the executive, engineer, salesman, organizer, or public relations man in a developing country like Lebanon.

Lastly, the relationship between enterprise and development, discussed earlier, the nature of which may even be intuitively discerned, must surely have concrete manifestations in the major and day-to-day decisions and acts of business leaders. The present study, among other things, aims at finding out how such concrete manifestations, even if not directly related to innovation, appear to the actors themselves. The views of business leaders and their scales of preference or priority in these areas of manifestation can indicate fairly well where the concentration of entrepreneurial interest and activity lies. They can also serve as some test of the degree of agreement between the theorist's definitions and scales of preference and those of the practitioner. The areas selected for examination are:

1) The idea of the business: its conception, elaboration, and the design of establishment embodying it (including technical and organizational design, choice of products, design of distribution system).

2) Provision of capital (both through self-financing and external financing).

3) Actual setting up of the establishment.

4) Formulation of policy regarding employment and coordination of productive resources.

5) Decisions regarding selling policy and methods, advertising, and opening up of markets.

6) Price and quantity determination.

7) Formulation of policy regarding relations inside the establishment including personnel organization, training of personnel, communication, and so on.

8) Formulation of policy regarding relations with partners, directors, or shareholders.

9) Formulation of policy regarding relations with the outside world: other establishments, banks, government, relatives, and the public at large (with regard to changes in products and tastes).

10) Day-to-day management of establishment.

11) Termination of the establishment (i.e., liquidation and winding-up of business).

The present study focuses attention on the business leader and his establishment simultaneously for the purpose of determining entrepreneurial manifestations in that working association and of determining the locus of enterprise within it. The record of establishments that embodied some historical entrepreneurial contribution but did not now have a man at the helm with authority to make decisions of an entrepreneurial nature was of little interest for our purposes and was not further pursued. Likewise, men with entrepreneurial qualities potentially capable of introducing innovations into their establishments, but whose establishments showed no sign of such innovation having been introduced, had no acceptable claim to be listed as entrepreneurs. In short, the necessary conditions for the appearance of an establishment on our list of entrepreneurs were, first, the embodiment in it of an entrepreneurial innovation, and second, the presence of a man qualified and authorized to make entrepreneurial decisions. The present study is not therefore one of entrepreneurs in the abstract any more than it is of establishments embodying innovations regardless of the qualities and authority of the men at the helm. It is one of *innovating enterprise* expressed by business leaders through the medium of operating establishments.

This approach is of practical, as well as conceptual, value. It lays emphasis on accomplishment in its insistence that an entrepreneur can only prove his bent and qualities through successfully introducing some innovation into an establishment with which he is associated. Obviously, he will be unable to do so — given his bent and qualities — unless he enjoys the authority to make entrepreneurial decisions. The study of entrepreneurship becomes therefore one of men as well as of institutions in that entangled, intimate relationship which necessarily arises from the making of decisions by these men — decisions that are of significance both for the institutions and the men alike.

The Form and Locus of Enterprise

The entrepreneurial function can take more than one form and be performed through intermediaries of various types. We must therefore look at the forms of business organization prevailing and determine where the locus lies within each.

The form that normally comes to the observer's mind first is that of entrepreneurship in establishments that are owned singly. The next form is that of compartmentalized, but collective or plural entrepreneurship, which is present in the partnership and the corporate form of business. Entrepreneurship by a team is a variation of compartmentalization, and it mostly refers to those less common cases where business organization is so highly developed and the distribution of responsibility so clear-cut that it is possible for each member of the entrepreneurial team to perform his own functions independently but at the same time in harmony with policy set by the team. This form of enterprise is characterized by, and associated with, a high degree of sophistication in organization and action and a line of entrepreneurial tradition not likely to be found in underdeveloped countries. It is therefore important to investigate the extent to which such organization has evolved in Lebanon and the readiness of business leaders to seek, and heed, the advice of their specialized departments and services — if they have any — or of such specialized services operating independently.

We also ought to ascertain whether or not entrepreneurship appears more frequently and fully in one sector of the economy than in others, and whether and in what ways it differs in its manifestations in the different sectors. It is neither wise nor safe to be dogmatic in identifying the sector in which the evolution of enterprise should come first for the furthering of development, although one can make a tentative identification on the strength of the implications for development and for enterprise itself of the attitudes characterizing each of the sectors.

There is general agreement regarding entrepreneurial attitudes. Industrialism is usually associated with the willingness and ability to plan for a long range, to go into long-term investment, to wait for the flow of returns, and to accept low profit margins on annual returns in preference to something larger but probably much shorter-lived. It also calls for more advanced technology, organization, coordination, and teamwork — qualities of value not only for the business undertaking itself but also for the economy at large.

Mercantile enterprise generally presents a different picture: preference for immediate high profits although they may contain little promise of continuity; less and shorter-term investment; the idea of "transactions" as against continuous processes; little advanced technology and therefore little to learn beyond being "clever"; not much teamwork or complex organization; a greater wariness of the future and therefore a greater desire for liquidity.

The agricultural entrepreneur, important as he is at an early stage of development, has not made a large contribution to the evolution of enterprise in underdeveloped countries.[15] This is probably partly due to the fact that the technology of agricultural activity is not as highly exacting in training and educational requirements as the technology of manufacturing or finance. It is probably also partly due to the characteristic conservatism of agriculturists and their abhorrence of change of habit, location, or technique.

In making decisions, a business leader in manufacturing, professional services, or transport is likely to fit into a middle course between the highly speculative mercantile innovator and the socially conservative agricultural innovator who is less willing to take high risks. He is also likely to season his daring with rationality and calculation. If so, he brings into enterprise assets of great value for decision-making and ultimately for development.

The financial business leader with funds for medium and long-term investment has a special contribution to make apart from that of innovation in his own field. His services are essential to all other business leaders, no matter in what sector they operate. This is true even with the rise in the degree of self-financing in corporations. The growth of a banking system is a necessary prerequisite for the growth of the various sectors in the economy. In its absence, credit will be prohibitively expensive, as the experience of underdeveloped countries generally shows.

Before my associates and I began interviewing business leaders we analyzed the sectors of agriculture, trade, industry, finance, and services in order to find out the manner in which entrepreneurial resources are allocated in Lebanon. After long debate, we decided to exclude the whole of the trade sector and parts of the services sector from the purview of the study.[16]

True, one can make an argument for including trade. If the contribution of a sector to national income is to be taken as indication of its contribution to the process and pace of development, surely trade, which is the source of more than one fourth of the national income of Lebanon, ought to be accorded the place of honor as a development-promoting sector, and enterprise in this sector ought to be studied with the greatest interest and attention. Furthermore, mercantile enterprise plays an important role in economic development by relieving manufacturing risks related to the introduction of new goods. Most manufacturing establishments in Lebanon produce commodities for the like of which an internal or transit market has already been established through the successful diffusion of imports in Lebanon, or of transit goods in neighboring countries. Thus, commercial enterprise establishes the tastes of consumers on the one hand, and provides a large part of the finance required for further ventures in manufacturing industry, banking, and agriculture, on the other hand. It follows that the mercantile entrepreneur in Lebanon is a predecessor of the industrial entrepreneur and a force behind his emergence.

On the other hand, most of the activity in the trade sector and certain parts of the services sector is very traditional and therefore noninnovational in character. Where certain innovational manifestations could be discerned — as in the successful introduction and promotion of a new perfume or shirt or of a new way of rendering some type of service — they seemed too distantly and tenuously related to development. For this reason, and in view of the limitations of time, qualified interviewers, and funds, the exclusion of trade and some services from this inquiry seems warranted.

An interesting point which, like the preceding one, also has a bearing on the origins and mobility of business leaders, is the ramification or spreading out of the activity of many leaders into two or more sectors, as well as into two or more industries within the same sector (indeed, in a few cases, into two or more establishments in the same industry). If its chronology and circumstances were to be examined carefully, and if it were found to be associated with the stages of success achieved by business leaders, this ramification might throw light on the valuation these men attach to various types of economic activity, on their notions of security and of success, on the urges and motives that make them act, and on the nature of interdependence among industries and sectors and how development may be affected by this interdependence. It could also be revealing with regard to the typology of enterprise.

Typology and Qualities of Entrepreneurs

Many typologies have been suggested in contemporary literature, and I will not attempt to add to the list.[17] Instead, I aim to look for predominating qualities from certain angles without a predetermined system of classification.

One of these angles is the extent of intuitiveness, calculativeness, "system," or sophistication in decision-making. This evaluation is close to Arthur H. Cole's "analytical" typology according to which entrepreneurs are empirical (or rule-of-thumb), rational (or informed), and cognitive (or sophisticated).[18] Another angle is the degree of specialization in entrepreneurship.[19] A third is that of daring or caution in innovation, and the extent of innovation, manifest in the readiness to introduce new products and methods of production, and so on. When the different sectors and forms of business organization are viewed from these several angles, the interesting variety of entrepreneurial qualities emerges. The results may arouse still greater interest when viewed against the background of entrepreneurial resources evolving within different business and cultural contexts.

At this point it becomes necessary to warn against a contradiction one is likely to fall into through adopting two incongruous positions simultaneously: the one affirming the inherent difference of entrepreneurial types manifest in the choice by different business leaders of different sectors to operate in; the other affirming the basic oneness of these types manifest in the active operation of the same business leader in different sectors simultaneously and his adoption of different forms of business organization for his varied establishments. Acceptance of the first position would be at variance with the reality of the ramification of the same leader's activity. Acceptance of the second position would amount to a negation of "pure" types. (The reconciliation of the two positions will be attempted when we come to the analysis of the empirical data in Chapter 4.)

Origins and Mobility of Business Leaders

Three broad questions about the origins of business leaders are worth examining for the detection of the association, if any, that exists between these origins and the types, qualities, and performance of the leaders in various sectors and activities.

The first question has to do with the national and denominational origins or groupings of entrepreneurs. In our investigation, we planned to identify the legal nationality (citizenship) of a respondent at the time of interviewing and to find out what his recent origin was (i.e., father's nationality at the time of the respondent's birth) and from what country he came, and under what circumstances. There are several large national and denominational groups in the business community including original Lebanese, Syrians, Armenians, Palestinians, and Kurds. They belong to the Christian, Moslem, Druse, and Jewish faiths. While it is likely that members of these groups have gone into all sectors in the economy, it would be interesting to detect any concentration that might exist.

The second question is the social and cultural origin or background. Here belong such matters as the respondent's social class, rural-versus-urban origin, family's traditional occupation, and affiliation with and activity in cultural and educational organizations. Here also belongs the important matter of religious denomination. As many questions relating to these matters as possible were to be pursued in subsequent interviewing.

We refused to approach this part of the inquiry with any rigid contentions regarding the social background of business leaders or the way in which the components of this background influence the type, qualities, and behavior of these men. They can conceivably come from every stratum in society.[20] Since the Industrial Revolution, a large number of different groups have performed the entrepreneurial function in one place or another. However, a good guess might be that the group broadly designated as the middle class, including (as it usually does in societies beginning to develop) the lower echelons of the upper, privileged classes, supplies society with the bulk of its entrepreneurial resources. To these must be added minority groups if they feel what might be called "cultural extraterritoriality" (that is, relative freedom from the repressive effect on enterprise of the local culture) and if their social and national background is not more repressive than their adopted milieu.

In discussing the influence of the social and cultural factor on the behavior of business leaders it ought to be remembered that these men are "never of the basic type"—they are rebels, or at least deviants, who do not feel chained to the urgings and taboos of their background, of their given situation. They are distinguished by being nonconformist in their business setting. Nevertheless, rebellion does not negate the influence of social and cultural background. Conceivably, it can occur within the border line of this background—indeed may even be reinforced by it, especially that part of it which is formed through education, training, and pre-entrepreneurial travel and experience.

The third question to be examined relates to training, education, and pre-entrepreneurial travel and experience. These largely define the direction and area of activity that follows them, the more so the more the entrepreneur is conscious of his stock of experience deriving from these sources.

In view of the long tradition of trade and craftsmanship in Lebanon it is of interest to find out whether, and how, the occupational background of merchants and artisans shows itself in the direction and manner of subsequent entrepreneurial activity. How often and how deep does the entrepreneur dip into ideas and practices learned in pre-entrepreneurial experience? How readily does he deviate from the pattern of products, markets, and processes familiar to him from that experience?

Apart from the origins of business leaders, their mobility between social groups and between economic sectors is a question worth examining. Through general observation, one sees a good deal of movement, with or without complete dissociation. As in many other underdeveloped countries, there is in Lebanon a wide diffusion of the activities that business leaders undertake, especially those in the trade and services sectors.

Preliminary documentary research for the drawing up of lists of respondents revealed that very frequently large import-export merchants also dealt in transit trade, clearance operations, shipping, overland transport, merchandise insurance, and perhaps in some contractual construction work and in finance on the margin. This phenomenon may result from an initial lack of specialization in training, from the desire to make up in variety of activities for the limitedness of growth within the firm, from the desire to spread business risks, or from the irresistible attractiveness of unused opportunities arising from the paucity of entrepreneurial resources. Though the present study was not designed to determine the operative causes in the case of Lebanon, it was meant at least to indicate the extent to which such diffusion prevails.

The Business Leader and His Environment

How does the business leader react to the level of economic activity and to the various economic facts and factors that influence economic life? How does he try to change any or all of these facts and factors to suit his purposes? How does he conceive of the effect of his role and actions on the facts and factors? These are some of the broad questions that need to be explored in connection with the relationship between the business leader and his economic milieu.

Doubtless, the level of economic activity is what it is only because business leaders, among other agents, behave in the way they do. But to ask about the effect of this level on entrepreneurial behavior is not begging the question since, given a certain level in period one, business leaders take certain attitudes and decisions influenced by that level which in turn influence the level in period two, by which they will be influenced in their decisions influencing the level in period three, and so on.

What should be sought with respect to such an influence is the reaction of business leaders to a number of factors, such as uncertainty of the future, input prices, and the condition of the market and its readiness for new products and new processes. The relationship between the entrepreneur and the "economic organization" ought also to be examined. It is important to ascertain his reactions to the state of business legislation, money and credit agencies, research facilities, training and skills, organizational forms of business establishments, the managerial and foreman classes, the labor force and trade unions, and market structure of inputs and products. Lastly, the businessman's sense of a business community and his solidarity with it, his sense of conformity or of rebellion, what he expects of this community and what he feels his obligations toward it to be, are matters worth investigating.

To say that political climate, including the condition of government and political attitudes, is a major influence in the entrepreneur's environment is to state the obvious. Yet it is essential to find out more specifically how the political factor influences Lebanese business leaders. How differently does it influence the time horizon of men in different sectors, or of different origins or backgrounds? How does it influence the allocation of talent between business and government?

An attempt must also be made to uncover what the business leaders themselves view as significant in their political environment. What, for instance, is their estimate of the effects of government action (or inaction, as the case may be) in the fields of business legislation, administration, monetary and fiscal policy, and social overhead investment? Do they feel there is inefficiency, corruption, lack of continuity in policy; and how do these influence business action? And, finally, what do business leaders ask of government?

Questions about the effect on the entrepreneur of the local culture are extremely difficult to answer, if only because the large number of community groups in the country have somewhat different cultural backgrounds and different degrees of sensitivity to the national cultural heritage. The task of defining and understanding the backgrounds of these groups, let alone postulating about the impact of these backgrounds, was beyond the resources at our disposal. The decision was therefore taken to keep the questions relating to the cultural factor at a bare minimum in the conceptual framework and in the questionnaire. The questions posed center mostly around social approval and the entrepreneur's valuation of different businesses. This, obviously, is an indirect and limited approach.

The Motives of the Entrepreneur

Motivation is another area the exploration of which is fraught with difficulty and danger. Nevertheless it was decided to examine its outer fringes at the point where the manifestations of deep-set motives become visible in actions and choices.

Attention first turns to the profit motive. An intriguing question here is the relative importance of the pecuniary motive as against nonpecuniary motives influencing the entrepreneur's actions.[21] Furthermore, specification as to the nonpecuniary motives prevailing — sense of achievement, power and status, acceptance and recognition, expansion, branching off into other industries or sectors, service to community — is interesting and instructive.

Two further questions of interest to the economic theorist are worth posing. The first deals with the minimum rate of profit considered adequate by the capital-owning business leader for his investment to remain where it is, and whether, on what conditions, and where the capital would move, if profit went below that rate. The second question deals with the nature of the business leader's reward — is it profit, wages, or interest, and for what function (or functions) does he consider it to be the reward? Some insight into the inner desires of the business leader with regard to his career and his satisfaction with it may thus be gained and may, in turn, point to social pressure and inner compulsion as motivating factors.

At the base of motivation is the system of values consciously or unconsciously espoused by the business leader. This system ultimately, though only partly, expresses itself in the choice that he makes of what he regards as indicators or manifestations of success worthy of pursuit, or as failings to be avoided. Here are some "success" indicators used in the inquiry:

1) Large profits, or the possession of a certain type and size of wealth.

2) Growth in the size of the establishment and in its operations, including buying out competitors.

3) Branching off into other fields of business activity.

4) Assurance of continuity in the business.

5) Increase in product variety.

6) Introduction of important technical improvements.

7) Change of form of business organization (e.g., from partnership to corporation).

8) Improvement in product quality, without necessarily expanding the size of business.

9) Helping entrepreneurial talent to emerge, that is, seeing former employees or associates emerge as entrepreneurs on their own.

10) Interest in, and contribution to, welfare, whether of one's labor force, family and relatives, or community, and whether for the purpose of charity or the promotion of knowledge.

The "failings" suggested were:

1) Ostentation in spending (or in investment).

2) Participation in politics (or aloofness from politics).

3) Long holidays (or short, or even no holidays).

4) Quick expansion in business (or contraction of business, or stagnation at the same size).

5) Branching off into other fields of business (or concentration on one field).

6) Career inconsistency.

7) Lack of planning.

"Rejuvenation" of the Entrepreneurial Spirit

How, and to what extent, do entrepreneurs avoid, counteract, or compensate for, the deterioration of their innovational activity into mere managerial routine? That is, how do they safeguard against running low in new ideas? The question is significant for the whole economy inasmuch as the drying up of innovation will threaten to curb the rise in the rate of growth made possible by the application of successful, innovating enterprise.

Certain processes and actions are likely to help in bringing about the process of "rejuvenation" of the entrepreneurial spirit, and are therefore worth investigating. They are:

1) Technical, organizational, and market research.

2) Acquaintance with the worlds of technology and business abroad, and willingness to learn from foreign experience through travel, visiting of fairs, reading of technical and business journals and books (both by the business leader and by his responsible staff).

3) Readiness to respond to the market's wishes — whether changing, anticipated, or existing but unsatisfied.

4) Internal originality: that is, the evolving of ways and means whereby new tastes can be "created" and their satisfaction provided for, new production or distribution methods and new markets can be found, or organization and technical processes can be improved.

5) The admission of "new blood" — men with fresh ideas, whether local or foreign, as business associates and senior assistants, or as independent operators.

With this last question the circle of the inquiry is completed.

It moves from the perception of an innovation at the very start to the conception of an establishment embodying the innovation and capable of profitably capitalizing on it, to the designing and actual setting up of the organization that will embrace all the fields of activity of the establishment and will determine the relationships within it and between it and its environment, to the determination of products and productive resources, to the setting of the machinery into motion, to the conquest of markets and the attainment of entrepreneurial motives, and finally to the admission of new ideas and new blood into the establishment.

An establishment may never introduce another innovation as important in quality or degree as the one which it embodied on coming into existence. Its greatest achievement may be to grow modestly in size and operations and to improve its products and services slightly. This is enough for most establishments. But the leaders, those who keep the economy growing fast and who help change its character, rarely find satisfaction in modest growth and slight improvement. No sooner is an innovation absorbed than they search for another that will enable their establishment to expand fast, or will require them to move into a new avenue altogether. They resist falling into a routine groove. The rejuvenation of their entrepreneurial spirit starts a new cycle in their activity. But here we part company with them.

Chapter 3

DESIGN AND CONDUCT OF THE STUDY

SELECTION OF RESPONDENTS

WHILE the conceptual framework, and later the questionnaire, was being prepared, a lengthy country-wide search was being conducted. It was a search for the business leaders to whom to put the questions — a search for sectors, businessmen's names, establishments, addresses. At the practical level, this assignment presented the greatest challenge of the study. With two, later three, assistants, I set out to find the sources of information likely to be of help in drawing the lists of potential respondents to be interviewed later. In addition to determining what these sources were, we had to evaluate the comprehensiveness and the reliability of the information, and to improve and supplement this information where necessary.

After some initial inquiries, it became clear that information of this kind must be mined from a variety of sources: from public and semipublic bodies and from individuals. The semipublic bodies, set up by the business community, that proved the most valuable were chambers of commerce, of industry, and of agriculture in the urban centers of Beirut, Tripoli, Zahle, Baalbek, Sidon, and Tyre. Next in usefulness were the syndicates or societies of engineers and of industrialists. The least useful were municipal councils, the records of which were not organized in a way that could contribute to our search.

From the records of the semipublic group of sources came the first information on establishments in the fields of transport, contracting, professional services (like insurance, auditing, consultation, advertising, research), finance, trade, agriculture, and manufacturing industry. Establishments in all these fields but the last two were registered in the chambers of commerce, if anywhere.

But the information was not in ready form, waiting to be collected. We had to review the files or card records of more than eight thousand establishments in order to pick out businesses that seemed to qualify as innovating establishments. More than one half of this large number had very lean files or card records containing skeletal information. This indicated that the establishments concerned had died since the record was made, had failed to renew their membership in the chamber or society, or had not furnished further information about themselves. In any case, the phenomenon indicated that the establishments had not acquired a position significant enough to justify keeping their membership alive and their file up-to-date. At the minimum, these lean files contained the name and address of the establishment, its legal form, the name or names of its owner or owners (or directors, if a corporation) and the persons empowered to sign for it, its registered capital, the capital rating given to it by the chamber (amounting to a status rating), and its objectives and field of operation.

Quite frequently the capital declared was larger than the capital rating suggested by the chamber; this inflation was probably an attempt to improve the standing of the establishment with the chamber and the business community. As frequently, the objectives and fields of activity stated were very broad, perhaps to allow flexibility. Under these circumstances it was quite difficult to determine the major lines of business for the purpose of classification of establishments by sector and subsector. Luckily, the officers of the chambers of commerce, agriculture, and industry possessed intimate knowledge of the activities of the business community. Their knowledge served as a first check on the correctness of data and in most cases led to the preliminary determination of the field of activity of major emphasis.

However, we accepted neither the data in chamber records nor the qualifications made by the officers, extremely informative and valuable as they were, as final and completely satisfying. In two fields of activity, the hotel business and manufacturing industry, we sought more complete and better organized data in records of two government departments: the Commissariat of Tourism and Resorts, and the Industry Section of the Ministry of National Economy. The first had all hotels arranged by class. It also had information on the capacity of hotels and the facilities and services offered. The second, in association with the Economic Research Institute of the American University of Beirut, had just finished an industrial census. We were able to examine the records (including the original questionnaires where necessary) of the 1861 establishments covered by the census and the questionnaires.[1]

Outside the hotel business and manufacturing industry, information was time and again solicited from a variety of sources, and checked for consistency and accuracy with small business and professional organizations and through direct contacts with established leaders in the fields concerned. The contacts were quite successful in the sense that the response was good and information was readily given. It can be safely said that the lists of businessmen to be interviewed in consequence emerged in as near a final and complete a form as possible.

There are two reasons for this result. First, by the time individual contacts and inquiries were under way and the lists were being prepared, we knew exactly what we were looking for. The specifications were precise and the terms used not too "academic" for the informants. Second, the established leaders contacted, being members of a small community, knew who was who in their own fields — indeed, they were very familiar with the innovational contributions of their competitors and therefore spoke with authority.

As a further measure of precaution, several individual checks thus undertaken were rechecked to remove all lingering doubts with regard to the soundness of the judgment or the comprehensiveness of the information received in earlier contacts. Such rechecks were mostly in the fields of agriculture, finance, and contracting, and to a lesser extent in those of professional services, tourism, and transport.

In this search for respondents, which lasted for about one year, what was sought was establishments that embodied some innovational idea (as defined earlier) and that built or improved an organization capable of successfully promoting the idea and assuring the businessman a position of leadership in the field. No bar was placed to the eligibility of women as entrepreneurs, but none qualified.

Finding the right respondents to interview was least difficult in the industrial sector, where records were adequate and informative, and where the novelty of most undertakings made the determination of the identity of innovators possible and often obvious.

Industry

The files of all 1861 manufacturing establishments were first sifted. The business leaders among them were singled out, district by district, industry by industry. Some 400 establishments were thus selected. Then followed a second round of elimination on the basis of size: all establishments with a labor force below 20 were dropped, with the exception of 25 pioneering establishments. These 25 were the innovators in their various fields and locality, and their elimination would have distorted the composition of the entrepreneurial group. By eliminating about 200 small-sized establishments we made our peace with expediency. None of the 200 dropped possessed any special merit to call for their inclusion in the selected group — none embodied innovations or organizational patterns more striking than those introduced by somebody in the group selected. During the process of rechecking immediately preceding the interviewing, about 58 other establishments were dropped, leaving 142. The number actually covered in the study (after refusals and final disqualification subsequent to interviewing) was 130.

Each one of the 130 businessmen at the head of these establishments had distinguished himself by introducing some significant innovation into industry. There were those who had taken on a traditional processing activity and transformed it into a full-fledged manufacturing industry operating under factory conditions. Examples are flour-milling, leather-tanning and shoe-making, food-processing and canning, and the production of furniture, confectionery, soap, oil, textiles (cotton, wool, and synthetic fiber), garments, pottery and ceramics, bricks, beverages (alcoholic and nonalcoholic), biscuits and macaroni, hardware, and glass.

There were also those who had launched into altogether new fields of production — phonograph records, cement, electricity, foam rubber and other rubber products, air-conditioners, liquid gas, sugar, pasteurized milk, plastics, machine tools, hangars, motorboats and trawlers, pressed wood and plywood, metal furniture, kitchen utensils, sanitary fittings, lithography, paints, fertilizers, antitank mines. Both traditional-turned-modern and altogether new activities used new machines and processes of production. Only in a small number of cases was the novelty restricted to a certain region in the country: the vast majority of the industrialists interviewed had introduced something new that was a duplication of nothing in existence elsewhere in Lebanon.

Where novelty in products or machines used was not in evidence, other equally important innovational contributions were. These belonged in the area of organization: in the internal design and structure of the establishment, in the professional services and communication mechanisms set up, or in external relations involving vertical integration or horizontal integration. More often than not establishments pioneering in products and processes were also pioneers in their organizational build-up.

Agriculture

Agriculture proved to be a specially difficult sector at the stage of list preparation. No one organization, public, semipublic, or private, had lists with a wide coverage of agricultural establishments, whether new or traditional. The preliminary investigation carried us to the Ministry of Agriculture, the chambers of agriculture, the rural experimental station of the French Technical Mission, the School of Agriculture at the American University of Beirut, the U.S. Operations (Point IV) Mission, and private agricultural engineers.

The list of innovators in agriculture had to be built up name by name, on the basis of the innovators' judgment of each other. Owing to the dispersion of agricultural establishments, these judgments proved much less adequate than those of industrialists, contractors, or bankers. Therefore, although we ended with only sixteen persons interviewed, we had to make many trips to all parts of the country and to talk to a dozen agricultural leaders before feeling that the list in hand was satisfactory. The final decision on names was made on the basis of the significance and magnitude of the innovation introduced and the organization built around it. A farmer introducing a new type of tomato, for instance, while keeping his operations at their former small scale within a traditional, family-type set-up, did not qualify to appear on the list. To have qualified he would have had to capitalize on the innovation by expanding his business and reorganizing production and marketing in a commercial way.

The sixteen men who qualified had large-scale, well-organized operations. All had introduced some new fruits or crops or new breeds of cattle, fowl, or pigs. Some had mixed farming; several had their own refrigeration or silo and storage facilities; a few had an efficient marketing organization of their own or had an integrated operation involving agricultural production, industry (like meat-packing or crate-making), and distribution. In a couple of cases we found serious research and experimentation with fruits or crops and with cattle and chicken breeding; in two other cases the emphasis was on large nurseries and flower beds. Invariably, the operation strove to be scientific and was well-planned — a market operation on a large scale quite distinct from that characteristic of the activity of the gentleman-farmer.

Finance

The scope for innovation in the financial sector proved on examination to be quite restricted. This limited the indicators of innovation used to compile our list. Furthermore, we faced three practical problems.

The first problem was the drawing of a dividing line somewhere through the large list of banks, banking houses, and the legion of small money-changing establishments that are no more than a hole in the wall but that have quite a high and profitable turnover. After a debate of some length, the decision was taken to ignore all establishments except those which were officially designated as "banks," having met certain minimal requirements in capital, reserves, and organization. The decision was thought tenable on two counts: (1) that these financial institutions differ from the traditional banking houses and money changers in the major respect of the novelty of organization; (2) that the operations of these banks are very large and therefore play a major role in the financing of the economy's transactions and the promotion of its growth.

The second practical problem concerned long-established foreign, or mixed foreign-and-Lebanese, banks. It was decided (though not until the interviewing had begun) not to include these banks because the authority for decision-making in significant matters resided outside Lebanon with ruling groups in foreign mother companies or principal offices. In more than one case it turned out that, although Lebanese citizens or residents owned shares in the capital, both the deciding vote and the real authority at the board level were neither *Lebanese* nor *in* Lebanon. All cases conforming to this pattern were disqualified.

After eliminating the smaller, traditional banking establishments and the foreign-controlled banks, we were left with some two dozen establishments, most of which were in Beirut, within a radius of about two hundred yards. Then we were faced with a third question. Was seniority on the basis of age of establishment — indicating an entrepreneurial lead — alone to qualify establishments for appearance on the list of respondents? Our answer to this question was no. Leadership in terms of seniority certainly entitled the leaders to selection. But latecomers also qualified if they catered to a new market; distinguished themselves through superior organization; opened up branches in centers not previously serviced by banks; pioneered in the extension of certain services like introduction of savings departments, the arranging of foreign accounts for clients, or the undertaking of hire-purchase operations; equipped themselves with modern accounting and other banking machinery; or set up research departments.

The questions answered, the list of qualifying banks was drawn. The number finally visited for interviews was fourteen. These included one establishment that was semipublic, in which private investors owned sixty per cent of the capital and the government forty per cent. It is the only bank that supplies medium- and long-term credit for industrial, agricultural, and real estate (mostly hotel) development, but none for mercantile purposes.

Services

As has already been mentioned, not all fields of activity in the services sector were examined. The following were thought worth inclusion owing to their direct contribution to the economic growth of the country: (1) The hotel business, which is a major earner of foreign exchange resources and in which substantial investment has been and continues to be made. We selected the pioneers in the field and the modern large hotels that offer a certain standard of services and facilities. The rating of the Commissariat of Tourism and Resorts was used as a basis for elimination. (2) Transport of passengers and of goods by land, sea, and air where an organization has been built around the service and where operations have grown beyond a certain modest size. (3) Contracting and speculative construction, both in public works like roads and bridges (customarily built by private firms for the government), and in private undertakings. This subsector includes housing societies or corporations which buy and develop land and build housing schemes for resale. (4) Professional services, including insurance, auditing, consultation, advertising, and research. In both (3) and (4) individual operators were excluded; only when the contractor or professional person had built an organization around his activities and these had grown in scale of operation beyond a certain minimum was he selected. In all cases under (2), (3), and (4) the class ratings of the chambers of commerce were used as a preliminary basis in the process of elimination.

Other fields of the services sector, such as entertainment, purely personal services, or intermediary services (like night clubs, beauty salons, bars, cafés and restaurants, cinemas, public baths, real estate agencies, and brokerage) were excluded from the purview of the study. Certain services like private schools and hospitals were excluded because their contribution to development is of very long-term effect, and, although most of them are highly lucrative undertakings, their avowed purpose is not profit-making.

Even more than in the case of agriculture we had in the case of services to go beyond the records and information of the chambers of commerce for the drawing up of the lists of respondents. The lists could only be prepared after numerous contacts with acknowledged representatives or leaders in the various fields of the services sector and after repeated checks and cross-checks. Finally lists carrying sixty-one names were drawn. Out of these eleven were disqualified during interviewing and three refused to be interviewed, leaving forty-seven accepted interviews.

The Final Selection

The following figures provide a picture of the whole operation of the search for respondents.

1) Files in the public and semipublic organizations which we surveyed contained information on over 8000 establishments in the sectors of trade, finance, services, agriculture, and industry. This number excluded (a) hotels and most of the subsectors in the services sector later excluded by us; (b) manufacturing establishments employing less than 5 workers, and larger establishments set up between the date of the industrial census and the end of 1958 (these last were later added by us); (c) workshops and small service and repair shops like garages, laundries, watch-repair shops, and so on; and (d) singly operated small businesses and small partnerships in the sectors of trade (especially retail), services, and finance whose owners believed there was little or no advantage for them in being members of chambers of commerce and other trade associations. Owing to the light it throws on the structure of the Lebanese economy, the raw information found in 3492 active files in the chambers of commerce and in 1861 files in the Industry Section of the Ministry of National Economy has been classified and tabulated by us. The classification is made according to the major field of activity, to the legal form of business organization, and (in the case of the 3492 establishments only) to the size or capital rating. The information appears in Tables A, B, and C in Chapter 4.

2) Out of the preliminary review of the files mentioned above and of the process of elimination already described, a tentative list emerged containing 375 potential respondents, divided as follows: 200 in manufacturing industry; 50 in agriculture; 25 in finance; 100 in services.

3) Further research and cross-checking resulted in the elimination of 132 names, mostly because of failure to qualify as business leaders, but in some cases because of duplication in the records.

4) The balance of 243 were designated for interview. Fourteen of these declining to cooperate, a total of 229 were interviewed.

5) Out of 229 interviews, 22 were finally disqualified for failure to meet our requirements adequately. The accepted interviews

which provided the data used in Chapter 4 totaled 207, divided as follows.

130 in manufacturing industry	or 62.80 per cent of total
16 in agriculture	or 7.73 per cent
14 in finance	or 6.76 per cent
47 in services	or 22.71 per cent

INTERVIEWING OF RESPONDENTS

Late in 1958, the conceptual framework of the study, the questionnaire, and the lists of establishments believed to embody innovational enterprise, were all ready. The time therefore came for the recruitment and training of interviewers (enumerators) and the pretesting of the questionnaire prior to actual interviewing. I selected eight research assistants — five young men and three young women — to help me conduct the interviews. All eight had college training, five of them in economics.[2] Four members of the force (three men and one woman) could conduct interviews in Arabic, English, or French, according to the choice of the respondent; the other four were all bilingual. (In a couple of cases when an Armenian respondent was fluent in nothing but Armenian, the services of an Armenian undergraduate student of economics were used.)

Intensive training was provided for the research assistants for one month. But before training began they were given substantial reading material on or around the subject of enterprise, including the paper on the conceptual framework of the study and the draft questionnaire. During the training period, interviewing techniques were discussed and the questionnaire was studied carefully and in detail, for the purpose both of achieving uniformity in the manner of posing and explaining questions, and of recording answers. The questionnaire was further examined for effectiveness: whether it was thought capable of providing answers to the questions raised in the conceptual framework, and whether these answers could be grouped together and quantified. The enumerators were to operate in teams of two. One member of each team was to put the questions to the respondent, the other member was to record the answers.

A second phase of training was started in January 1959. It coincided with the pretesting of the questionnaire. Eighteen respondents were interviewed, mostly by the author, in the presence of all or most of the eight research assistants. All those participating recorded the answers. These answers were later examined and compared at length, and discrepancies were explained and corrected. When the discrepancies were caused by ambiguity and open-end questions, the questionnaire was corrected.

Several respondents interviewed during this pretesting process proved ineligible as innovating entrepreneurs, and their questionnaires were subsequently disqualified. The others were contacted again after the questionnaire had been put in final form.* Their answers to the questions that had been altered were obtained and incorporated into their questionnaire forms.

In every single case, investigation was made beforehand, both in the establishment and outside it, in order to identify the proper person to be interviewed: the person who exercised the authority for entrepreneurial decisions in the establishment. Once found, it was he who was contacted regarding the interview. A letter was always sent out to the potential respondent informing him of the study and explaining its purposes, and requesting an appointment for an interview.† The letters were delivered by hand. A few days later, contact was made for the arrangement of an appointment. The letters went out under my signature as director of the Economic Reasearch Institute. This institute was known to the business community and respected by it, both because it formed part of the university and because of the numerous important studies it had undertaken concerning the Lebanese economy. After each interview, the questionnaire of the respondent was discussed

* The revised questionnaire is reproduced in Appendix B. It appeared in *Business History Review*, Spring 1960, pp. 98–110, and is now reprinted with the permission of that periodical.

† The letter is reproduced in Appendix A.

by the team. Whenever doubt arose with regard to the eligibility of the respondent (or of the establishment) as a business leader (or as an embodiment of innovational enterprise), the case was brought to me for discussion and final decision.

The interviewing was completed in the middle of July 1959. I took part (either as enumerator or recorder) in 35 out of the 207 accepted interviews, apart from those disqualified during the pre-testing stage. On the average, each interview took just under two hours.

On the whole, the reaction of the business leaders contacted was very friendly. Only 14 refused to participate; the rest cooperated hospitably and with frankness. This can perhaps be explained as a result of four factors: the study was conducted under the auspices of the American University of Beirut; the novelty of the experience to the overwhelming majority of respondents aroused their curiosity; in the request for an appointment, the significance of the study was pointed out and the fact duly underlined that only a select group of business leaders was to be interviewed, of which the person addressed was a member; the business leaders approached were obviously courteous by nature. Soon after the preliminary questions were over, the respondents usually warmed up to the interview and indicated a keen interest in the questions and in the study as a whole. In many cases, they went beyond the questions to impart further information about their background or experience.[3]

During the interviewing period, we began to edit the completed forms and prepare a "code." After being coded, the information was punched on cards, and the sorting and tabulation operations were finally undertaken. The straight tabulation resulted in 133 tables. Another set of 339 tables were prepared upon the cross-tabulation of significant dependent variables with several independent variables. The cross-tabulations were grouped as follows.

1) Age of respondent.
2) Family status (with regard to marriage and children).
3) Sector in which the major activity of the establishment falls.

4) Participation of respondent in other establishments in certain specified forms.

5) Form of capital ownership in establishment (i.e., form of business organization).

6) Education of respondent.

7) Religious affiliation of respondent.

The entire set of 472 tables has been made available elsewhere.* The analysis in the following chapter is based on information obtained from them. In the examination and use of these tables no elaborate statistical manipulation has been attempted. It was felt that the nature of the information called simply for the calculation of frequency distributions and of proportions. The cross-tabulations establish associations between variables; no attempt was made to ascertain functional relationships, for these can be sought legitimately only in the complex of several variables acting on each other. We have tried to make sense out of such entangled patterns of causation through the analysis of data from several cross-tabulations, once these have been examined individually. The grouping of findings is therefore analytical, not statistical. Inferences drawn from the findings are presented in Chapters 4 and 5.

One last word may be in order regarding the coverage of the questionnaire. Admittedly, with such a wide area explored, no one point can receive more than brief attention. Would it not have been better to have designed the study in a way permitting more concentration on a fewer points in the inquiry? This legitimate question would have been answered in the affirmative had the type of study undertaken been one of many like it. As this is probably the first country-wide, all-sector empirical study of entrepreneurship, it seemed advisable to aim at a very broad area of investigation in an effort to get the general bearings, rather than at a few specific points in an area still largely unmapped.

* See Appendix C for list of these tables and explanation of where they may be found.

Chapter 4

ENTREPRENEURS OF LEBANON: A SELF-PORTRAIT

In the whole formulation of concepts so far, the point of departure has been that of the observer, the student of theory. The interviews conducted for the present study sought the views and attitudes of business leaders in Lebanon in relation to a wide variety of issues. Presentation of the more significant findings in this chapter will reveal a self-portrait sketched by the business leader, against the portrait sketched in Chapter 2 by the theorist.

There will be confrontation between several areas of the two portraits. These are: the entrepreneurial function and the form and locus of enterprise; the origins and mobility of the business leaders interviewed; the mainspring of innovation; the quality of enterprise in Lebanon; the motives of enterprise; and the business leader and his environment.

THE BUSINESS LEADER, HIS FIRM AND HIS FUNCTION*

The entrepreneurial group in Lebanon is not representative of the total business community. The activities and experience of the

* The findings in this section are based on Tables 1–3, 7–12, 16, 18, 22–30, 106, 118, 134–137, 144–147, 151, 152, 221, 281–286, 320, 327, 338–342, 402, 419, 422, 424–429, 467. See Appendix C for list of Tables 1 through 472 and explanation of where they may be found.

Table A. Establishments registered at the Beirut Chamber of Commerce distributed by type of activity and by form of ownership[a]

Type of activity	*Single ownerships*	*Partner-ships*	*Corpora-tions*	*Total*
Trade in combination with commission agencies, transit trade, manufacturing, contracting, or insurance	483	242	22	747
Trade	1444	923	39	2406
Advertising, publishing, and printing	12	5	—	17
Insurance	—	—	1	1
Transport (passengers and freight)	26	14	4	44
Engineering works, contracting	166	20	3	189
Finance in combination with trade, manufacturing, or insurance	2	2	1	5
Banking and money exchange	3	12	20	35
Other services	24	12	12	48
Total	2160	1230	102	3492

[a] This table, compiled directly from the active files of the Beirut Chamber of Commerce during 1957–58, covers well over three quarters of Lebanon's establishments in the categories listed. For industry see Table C.

members of this group are probably of narrower scope than those of the whole community, but more significant for the economy. For business leaders innovate, in contrast to other businessmen who merely fit into established patterns of technology, organization, and products.

Several notable differences separate the group from the total business community, as can in part be seen from a comparison of the data in Tables A, B, and C with similar data relating to the group of 207 entrepreneurs. The first difference is in the structure of their activities. Though trade attracts the vast majority of business-

Table B. Establishments registered at the Beirut Chamber of Commerce distributed by type of activity and by capital grading[a]

	Grades						
Type of activity	*"A"*	*1*	*2*	*3*	*4*	*5*	*Total*
Trade in combination with commission agencies, transit trade, manufacturing, contracting, or insurance	4	62	68	274	250	89	747
Trade	13	185	343	857	658	350	2406
Advertising, publishing and printing	—	—	1	9	6	1	17
Insurance	1	—	—	—	—	—	1
Transport (passengers and freight)	2	6	4	6	14	12	44
Engineering works, contracting	—	8	16	88	59	18	189
Finance in combination with trade, manufacturing, or insurance	—	2	2	1	—	—	5
Banking and money exchange	13	10	8	4	—	—	35
Other services	3	7	3	12	16	7	48
Total	36	280	445	1251	1003	477	3492

[a] This table was compiled directly from the active files of the Beirut Chamber of Commerce during 1957–58. The grades are in a descending order of the size of capital, from "A" downwards, in accordance with the classification used by the chamber. The capital ranges of the grades vary widely from one type of activity to another; consequently they are not specified in the headings of the table.

men in the community, the 207 business leaders are mostly engaged in industry (130), while services (47), agriculture (16), and finance (14) follow at a distance. Trade, the most prevalent activity in the country, is also the least innovational.

The second difference is in the form of business ownership. In the business community at large, individual proprietorship is found in some three fifths of establishments, followed by the partnership

Table C. Manufacturing and mining establishments surveyed in the 1955 industrial census of Lebanon, distributed by locality, form of ownership, and industry[a]

By locality		*By form of ownership*	
Beirut District	995	Single ownership	1129
Mount Lebanon District	480	Partnership	694
North Lebanon District	241	Corporation	38
South Lebanon District	57	*Total*	1861
Beqa'a District	88		
Total for Lebanon	1861		

By industry	
Mining and quarrying	68
Food manufacturing, excluding beverages	554
Beverages industries	74
Tobacco manufacturing	3
Textiles	113
Footwear, wearing apparel, and other made-up textiles	245
Wood and cork manufactures, excluding furniture	71
Furniture and fixtures	168
Paper and paper products	16
Printing, publishing, and allied industries	108
Leather and leather products, excluding footwear	45
Rubber products	15
Chemicals and chemical products	37
Nonmetallic mineral products	153
Basic metal industries	3
Metal products, excluding machinery and transport equipment	102
Machinery, excluding electrical	23
Electrical machinery, appliances, and supplies	10
Transport equipment	10
Miscellaneous manufacturing	43
Total	1861

[a] Establishments set up after the census and before the present study was undertaken do not appear in this table, but were taken into account in choosing the 130 industrial establishments included in our study.

Source: Collated from Tables 1, 2, and 20 in: Republic of Lebanon, Ministry of National Economy, *Industrial Census 1955* (Beirut, 1957; mimeographed).

in over one third. Conversely, in the entrepreneurial group it is the partnership that leads, followed by individual proprietorship, the proportions being just under two fifths and just under one third, respectively. But what is more arresting is the relative popularity of the corporation. Whereas only 2.6 per cent of the establishments in the community are corporate, 28.5 per cent of those in the entrepreneurial group are corporate. This difference in form of ownership is probably a reflection both of the desire of the innovating to move away from traditional toward new forms, and of the greater appropriateness of these forms for the type of activity and scale of operations undertaken by the innovating.

Third, the group not only excels the community in average level of education but also includes noticeably larger proportions of men with undergraduate training and with graduate or professional training. Finally, the group differs from the community in the distribution of members by religious affiliation; specifically, a larger proportion of the business leaders are of the Christian faith. Indeed, in both religion and level of education, the entrepreneurial group presents a structure quite unlike that of not only the whole business community but also the whole population.

The Men and the Establishments

What kind of men are these business leaders? What kind of activities and establishments give expression to their innovational ideas? These are the broad questions to which answers were sought.

The 207 respondents are mostly middle-aged and over, two thirds being over 40 and two fifths over 50 (that is, at the time of interviewing in 1959). Those from 50 to 59 constitute the largest single age group, numbering 63 men; the next largest age groups are the forties and thirties. There are, however, 16 respondents between 20 and 29 years old. Only a few of these very young men are sons or business-heirs-presumptive of leading businessmen; the majority are pioneers in their own right. Although by and large the respondents are not young now, the majority of them started their entrepreneurial career rather young — between 25 and 35. Indeed, about 70 per cent of all the respondents started their career after the Second World War.

The establishments are mostly under 40 years of age. Over six sevenths of them have been set up since the end of the First World

War, and almost half since the Second World War. The wartime half-decade 1940–1944 produced a lag in the emergence of establishments embodying entrepreneurial innovations; fewer such establishments were started during that period than in any other half-decade since 1920. Furthermore, fewer business leaders started their careers during the war years than in any other half-decade since 1925. Were it not for this interruption, the youthfulness of business leaders at the outset of their careers would be even more marked.

When the age of the respondents is associated with their economic sector, the most striking fact is the tendency of the youngest men to be in industry, rather than in agriculture, finance, and services.[1] Almost all those under 30 years old are in industry.

Concerning the financing of establishments, information could not be obtained on the *size* of capital, both at the start of business and at the time of interviewing, but some information was obtained on the *sources* of capital. Over three fourths of the answers to questions on sources indicated reliance by the respondents on their own resources in financing their businesses (or in financing their personal participation in share-capital, if their establishments were corporations). The rest indicated reliance on bank loans and on borrowings from nonrelatives and relatives. In over 61 per cent of the cases where resources came from previous business activities they had come from trade; the balance came from nonbusiness sources, broadly grouped under "family resources." Inheritance was the most significant among these, followed by personal savings, gifts from parents or other relatives, sale of property, and other sources. There is good reason to believe that a part of the item "gifts," as well as of the larger unspecified item "other sources," is in fact dowry brought to the respondents by rich wives. But the questionnaires and tables do not say anything on this point.

It has already been pointed out that the partnership leads among the forms of ownership of establishments, followed by the single ownership and the corporation. Contrary to what one might expect, the corporate group included more men in their sixties than in their twenties. The following schematic ranking of the three forms of ownership* reveals the prevalence of each form in relation to age. The age group is given at the left. In the right-hand columns, the forms of ownership are ranked in descending order from left to right. P stands for Partnership, S for Single (individual proprietorship), and C for Corporation.

20–29	P	S	C
30–39	P	C	S
40–49	S	C	P
50–59	S	C	P
60–69	C	S	P
70 and over	P	—	—

There may be several causes of this phenomenon. Business leaders not yet firmly established in the market do not have the prestige required to mobilize funds for the capital of a corporation from a large group of subscribers. Or, given their inexperience, business leaders may be hesitant to build up a corporate organization involving the creation and steering of a board of directors. Or, yet, young men may have a strong desire to be independent and to act alone or only in association with a small group of young friends. These efforts at explanation are tentative, but they fit the pattern visible in the ranking just made where the corporation moves from third, to second, to first position as age of respondents rises.

No fewer than 44 of the total of 59 corporations are under 16 years of age. No corporations were established during the years 1940-1943, and more than half of the 15 prewar corporations owed their appearance to the joint effort of Europeans and Lebanese, or to the fact that incorporation was the appropriate form of organization for the type of business undertaken (as in the case of electric power production). Taken together, 33 of the 59 corporations are in industry, and over two thirds of these were established after 1944. Services claim 15 corporations, finance 10, agriculture only one.

This pattern is understandable. One is bound to be impressed

* Adapted from Table 137, listed in Appendix C.

by the large number of corporations in manufacturing, which requires less capital than financial firms, and which is a more recent arrival in Lebanon than trade and services. The very newness of manufacturing activity, however, explains the presence of 33 corporations there; an entrepreneur is likely to "import" the shell along with the substance, the form of organization as well as the new type of activity. As for the financial sector, its 10 corporations make up a higher proportion of establishments (70 per cent) than is found in any other sector. Here the explanation is simply that banks require large capital and can best get it through the corporate form.

The Entrepreneurial Function

The respondents were asked: "As the person taking important decisions in the Establishment, what do you conceive your function or functions to be?" They were given a list of thirteen functions (to which they could add if they wished) and were requested to indicate the four most important functions in the order of their importance.[2]

The 207 entrepreneurs cast a total of 789 votes, some voting for fewer than four functions. More than half the total vote went to the following five functions.

Designing the organization (administration of various processes of production, marketing, research, etc.)	98 votes
Conception of the idea of the business	83
Management of establishment (day-to-day)	82
Technical decisions (choice of machines, processes, etc.)	71
Provision of capital	69

Even more important than the summation of the total vote was the order of importance in which the respondents viewed them. The ranking, regardless of age group, level of education, or of any other independent variable, produced the following results.

Highest frequency for first choice: Conception of the idea of the business (in 66 cases).

Highest frequency for second choice: Designing the organization (in 35 cases).

Highest frequency for third choice: Designing the organization (in 26 cases); Decisions regarding selling policy and methods, and advertising (in 25 cases).

Highest frequency for fourth choice: Price and quantity determination (in 32 cases).

The runner-up as first choice was "designing the organization," but it was marked in only 27 cases. This fact and the fact that the same function got the largest vote as second choice as well as third choice is indicative of the attention given to it at different levels in the scale of preference. The third and fourth choices were both closely contested by other functions. Obviously, the respondents were unmistakably clear in their opinion of the first choice, rather clear in their opinion of the second choice, but almost on the point of indifference between two functions when they came to the third and fourth choices.

Examination of the ranking of functions in association with the age groups and the level of education of respondents and with the sector and form of ownership of establishments reveals a few conclusions worth reporting.

1) To begin with, business leaders between 30 and 69 years of age awarded the largest vote to "conception of the idea of the business" as first choice. But the youngest respondents (20–29) placed most emphasis on management, and this is perhaps the most surprising thing in the pattern. About half of the men in the 20–29 group have been associated with their establishments since founding, with strong evidence that they themselves had conceived the idea of the business. Not choosing "conception of the idea of the business" for first place may mean that they underestimate the significance of what they have done, being still too close to the act to see it in its right perspective. Or it may mean that they are now so immersed in the management and organization tasks that follow the setting-up of business that they ignore the first landmark in their entrepreneurial careers. It is also possible that their start, being so recent,

has had the advantage of being preceded by the building up of some entrepreneurial tradition, to the point where innovation expressed in new establishments has been easier for them than it was for the older groups. Being easier, it does not seem exceptional.

2) When the views of respondents concerning the entrepreneurial function are related to the level of education, the only clear result is that "conception of the idea of the business" was first choice at all levels except that of 4–6 years of schooling. Beyond the point of first choice, there is no apparent pattern.

3) In each of the four economic sectors, "conception of the idea of the business" was chosen as the foremost function. Further down in the ranking of functions, the emphasis in industry and agriculture was on technical decisions, choice of product, and selling and markets, whereas in the finance and services sectors the emphasis was on management, employment and coordination of productive services, and organization.

4) In all three forms of ownership, "conception of the idea of the business" was selected by respondents as first choice among the functions. Other choices further down the scale indicate men in partnerships are more concerned with organization and management than are individual proprietors, and men in corporations more than in either of the other forms. Furthermore, a pronounced feature is the attention given to "provision of capital" in the individual proprietorship and partnership — a reflection of the fact that provision of capital is more relevant to analysis based on form of ownership than to that based on age, schooling, or sector.

Some general observations now can be made on entrepreneurial functions. The conviction with which the respondents selected their number one function shows how much they value new ideas: indeed, their views signify a characterization of entrepreneurship as the unearthing of good ideas for new types of business. The innovation involved embraces the whole idea of the business; it is not innovation in one narrow segment of that business such as technical processes, organization, or advertising. Focus on innovation in one segment would reflect a more discriminating attitude and a more sophisticated level of entrepreneurship than that encountered in Lebanon. This lack of discrimination has significant implications. In the great majority of cases, even when the respondents were articulate, intelligent, and highly educated, their answers were very broad. Thus their thinking of a whole business as being an embodiment of an innovation falls into a pattern with their failure — in replying to another question — to describe with precision their innovational contribution to the establishment. Furthermore, in most instances (particularly in finance and services), the respondents limited their view of innovation to physical changes, thus largely overlooking organizational, intangible changes in the establishment. This obsessive awareness of novelty in the establishment itself, or in the goods produced, received repeated confirmation during the study.[3]

There is, lastly, a conclusion which is drawn not from the aggregate body of tabulated data but from a perusal of individual questionnaires. There was a tendency for individuals to relate their choice of leading function to the particular phase of life of the establishment at the moment of interviewing, and to the nature and duration of their experience with the establishment. Thus, other things being equal, business leaders in long-established concerns seem to attach more significance to their function in introducing innovations of value in the everyday life and work of the establishment, such as selling, research, or technical improvement, than to the conception of the original idea. On the other hand, in newly started concerns — so prevalent in Lebanon — they seem to place most emphasis on conception of the idea; and this is the truer the more closely associated they are with such conception.

Furthermore, the immediate pressures and crises uppermost in the awareness of the respondent help to determine the respondent's answer, and the answer reflects what he believes to be his most effective role in relieving the pressures or meeting the crises. Thus, in an establishment that has been losing markets to its competitors, the business leader is likely to be concentrating attention on innovation and improvement in selling and advertising, and therefore to emphasize aggressive selling policy as a very important aspect of the entrepreneurial function. Likewise, in an establishment that is falling behind technically, the business leader is likely to emphasize the importance of technical innovation — the very thing that worries him most at the moment. And so on in other directions.

But no matter what phase of life or current experience the establishment is going through, and no matter how strongly the respondent is aware of the moment's crisis, his actual role in implementing the solution depends to a considerable extent on the degree of sharing of entrepreneurial responsibility in the establishment and the respondent's place in that system of sharing.

Locus of Authority in the Establishment

As previously stated, the entrepreneur is the man in whom the power to take entrepreneurial decisions *effectively* resides; he need not be the titular head of the establishment.[4] This definition permits the finding of a number of entrepreneurs in a single establishment, but in our investigation only one person per establishment was interviewed. Owing to the pressure of time and to the heavy costs of interviewing, the small number of other persons wielding some entrepreneurial authority had to be left out, although their presence and role were duly recorded. The respondents interviewed included chairmen and members of boards of directors in corporations, partners in partnerships, owner-managers in individual proprietorships, and executives owning no capital in all three forms of ownerships. In all cases the guiding principle for eligibility was the ability of the man interviewed to make major entrepreneurial decisions for and on behalf of the establishment. He could be an engineer, a public relations man, or the comptroller. In practice, however, it was found that all the respondents except 5 were right at the top of the hierarchy. But being at the top in 27 cases meant being head executive without owning capital. (Four of these 27 were priests running industrial undertakings on behalf of their religious orders.)

Specialists proved to be quite rare in positions of top or senior entrepreneurial authority. This situation is probably no different from that in most other underdeveloped countries where the specialist or expert is not allowed a great deal of authority in the implementation of his suggestions. Entrepreneurial ideas that come from the man at the very top have a much better chance of being introduced.

The business leader in Lebanon (like his colleagues in the Arab world and possibly in other underdeveloped regions) tries to keep in his own hands a vast amount of authority on a large number of matters, even when he cannot possibly handle them all properly. Quite often he is not aware of his shortcomings. In any case, he is jealous of his authority and will not give up part of it easily to senior assistants, especially those with technical training who are likely to have minds of their own. Indeed, over two thirds of the respondents frankly stated that nobody else below them in the hierarchy enjoyed power of an entrepreneurial nature. In the 66 cases (31.9 per cent) where respondents declared the existence of senior staff empowered to make entrepreneurial decisions, investigation showed that this power did not reach very far. There were always severe limitations on its exercise or continual interference in its use. This generalization applies whether the man in charge is capital-owning or non–capital-owning, but more when he is capital-owning.

Much more delegation of entrepreneurial authority takes place in finance and services than in industry and agriculture. The explanation may lie in the forms of ownership. Unlike industry and agriculture, banks are mostly corporations, a form in which division of labor in the entrepreneurial-managerial pyramid is more "accepted." When the association between delegation of authority and form of ownership is examined, clear evidence emerges that business leaders in corporations have a much greater tendency to share their authority with senior staff than business leaders in partnerships or in single ownerships.

The level of education of respondents seems to have a direct and positive relation to the delegation of authority. The proportion of those who delegate rises consistently with the rise in the years of schooling — with small exceptions. The principal exception is that men with graduate and professional training show a little less tendency to delegate than men with undergraduate training. It is just possible that the superior education of the top group makes them feel capable of handling the whole range of their major responsibilities single-handed. The data provide no better clue.

There is another level at which authority can be shared: this is horizontal sharing among equals, in contrast to vertical sharing with subordinates. The investigation showed that in just about two thirds of the cases the business leader shares his authority with partners or with colleagues of the board, or with the capital-owners if he is a salaried executive. The sharing takes several forms, singly or in combination. By far the most recurrent is that of joint decisions, followed distantly by that of division of areas of responsibility.

The majority of cases where the respondent shared his authority with nobody at his level were found in individual proprietorships; some cases were in partnerships, and a few in corporations. Lebanese corporate law stipulates that the board of directors is the highest operating authority. Therefore, the claim by some managing directors that they share authority with none must be understood in a pragmatic, possibly boastful, rather than a formal, sense.

The respondents were asked if they thought it advisable for an establishment to have as head a person who does not own part of its capital. A surprisingly large number answered in the affirmative —61 men, or 29.5 per cent of the total. This number is more than twice that of the respondents who do not own any capital in the business. If the fact be taken into account that some of the executives who own no capital answered the question in the negative, and that therefore an even larger part of the affirmative answer than appears at first sight came from capital-owning respondents, the impressiveness of the result becomes quite commanding. This result suggests that not a small number of business leaders in Lebanon believe that merit based on entrepreneurial ability is more essential for the assumption of responsibility in the establishment than the ownership of capital alone. Such a view was confirmed earlier during the investigation of the ranking of entrepreneurial functions, where "provision of capital" as one of the functions ranked very low.

The respondents in the youngest age group, 20–29, were the least tolerant of the holding of top entrepreneurial responsibility by someone who did not own part of the capital of the establishment, while the 60–69 group were just as strongly in favor. The only satisfying explanation of the contrast appears to be that as the experience and maturity of business leaders grow, so does their appreciation of talent as against the mere ownership of capital. Tolerance is also strangely low at the two extremes of education. So far as different forms of ownership are concerned, the highest level of tolerance is in corporations, the lowest in partnerships.

The next issue to be considered in connection with the flow of responsibility within the establishment is that of communication. The respondents were asked their views about the significance of the role of foremen (or supervisors, or chief clerks, as the case may be). Over two thirds of the respondents thought the function of foremen necessary for efficient operation, and another one fourth thought that the function — while necessary — depended on the size of business, because in a very small business the entrepreneur or manager could discharge it himself. Nobody said foremen are unnecessary. The overwhelming appreciation in theory of the function of the foreman is reflected in the fact that about two thirds of the establishments examined have their administration divided into sections or departments; this is especially true in corporations and among the more educated respondents. But in practice, the function of the foreman is generally underestimated, as excessive centralization of authority by top executives indicates.

No very clear pattern emerges from attempts to correlate the answers to the question on foremen with the sector of the respondent. The greatest frequency of votes in appreciation of the foreman's role appeared in finance, with agriculture, industry, and services following in that order. Being somewhat inconclusive, these results call for some explaining. The lead of the finance sector is probably a reflection of the formality of administration and the size of operations, both of which necessitate a good system of communication. In the case of agriculture, an effective supervisory system is required because of the low level of literacy and training of the labor force and — a less charitable explanation — perhaps because of the occurrence of some entrepreneurial absenteeism. Two points help to explain industry's lack of appreciation of the foreman. The first is the relative smallness of a number of the manufacturing establishments investigated. And second, many of the manufacturers had been artisans and operators of small workshops which grew slowly into what they now are. Thus these men betray a marked left-over of the attitudes and opinions associated with the small workshop, including the conviction that the entrepreneur personally must interest himself in the communication function and that nobody else can discharge this function as efficiently and effectively. The two points supplement each other.

Diffusion of Entrepreneurship in the Economy

The last question to consider with respect to the form and locus of enterprise is that of the diffusion of the activities of business leaders and the resultant dovetailing and interconnection between sectors and industries. Diffusion was measured through the direct participation of respondents in other establishments. A respondent was considered to participate "directly" in other establishments if he was: (a) an outright owner of an individual proprietorship; (b) a partner in a partnership; or (c) a chairman or a member of the board of a corporation.

As many as 119 of the respondents declared direct participation in 330 other establishments. Another 3 men declared participation but declined to indicate its nature or to state the number of establishments involved. This reticence is not nearly as surprising as the openness of those other respondents who not only answered the initial question in the affirmative but went on to list the establishments in which they participated and to indicate the nature of their participation. At the upper extreme of frankness was the respondent who listed 18 establishments; when asked why he stopped there he replied that his memory was not as good as it used to be.

The most frequent form of participation was membership (including chairmanship) in boards of directors of corporations. This is an interesting finding because it reveals interlocking directorates in corporations at a level that must be considered high for a country with a small number of corporations and with a passionate individualism manifested in privacy and secretiveness in business.

The interlocking is all the more compact because most of it occurs within a narrow circle of establishments. This fact points to what one might call "internal leavening." Fortunately for the economy, the process is spreading and the inner core seems to have reached out into different sectors, industries, and localities. The impression gained from interviewing suggests the conclusion that entrepreneurial resources in Lebanon can now safely be assumed to be capable of widening the reach of their leavening effect to the whole economy. To borrow from the broader terminology of economic development, we can say that entrepreneurs can now assure the economy a "sustained growth" within their ranks and from their own resources, given the present environmental setting.

BACKGROUND AND MOBILITY *

Like migrant birds, Lebanese businessmen instinctively follow the call of clement business climate. Adventurous and dynamic, they are awed neither by strange lands nor by foreign tongues. The joint legacy of their Phoenician and Arab ancestry is in unmistakable evidence. Whether settling in Carthage millennia ago, or in Dakar, Sydney, Detroit, or Kuwait today, the Lebanese manifest very much the same qualities.

At home as well as abroad, they are restless. They are very sensitive to the appeal of economic opportunity, therefore highly mobile. The visitor to Lebanon is immediately struck by the briskness of

* The findings in this section are based on Tables 11–16, 38–42, 52–58, 64, 65, 93, 127–131, 140, 150, 162, 165–168, 174, 175, 226, 231, 232, 237, 241, 242, 247, 255, 264, 277, 280, 289, 329–332, 345–347, 364, 420, 421, 470, 471. See Appendix C for list of Tables 1 through 472 and explanation of where they may be found.

life. In this general bustle, economic activity sets the pace. Movement is continuous across the frontiers of social classes and economic sectors. In the circumstances, a clear and stable social and economic pattern is extremely difficult to find.

The movement takes many forms. A Lebanese rarely finishes his days in the village of his birth. This is especially true of the businessman, attracted from his village by the greater opportunities of the cities. And the inhabitants of cities tend to gravitate toward Beirut, the capital, on achieving a certain degree of success. On succeeding further, they open branches or otherwise extend their operations first in Lebanon, then in Syria, Iraq, Jordan, Saudi Arabia, the Persian Gulf, or Iran.[5] At some point in their career they make their peace with liquidity and safety by putting a nest egg in a Swiss bank or by buying some gilt-edged security in the United States or Western Europe.

In the process, they also move from trade into contracting, finance, industry, real estate, or the hotel business. Their bare, unostentatious office is transformed into a more spacious one, with filing cabinets, clerks, and a secretary. Their local bank account is transferred from the small *maison de banque* which offers easy terms but insufficient security to one or more of the big solid banks where it goes through a variegated experience of abundance and over-draft, and where it changes form rapidly from Lebanese pounds to Swiss francs, to sterling, to dollars, as the occasion requires.[6]

The associations of our businessman also change. From a lone wolf operating single-handed he turns into a trusting partner, or into a gregarious shareholder in a corporation. Since he often has direct participation in two or more other concerns, the likelihood is great that he becomes all these types simultaneously. Being versatile he is ready to change industry or occupation, form of organization or locale, as business opportunity demands or the specter of the tax collector necessitates. Yet he retains his basic qualities.

These qualities are somewhat contagious. The non-Lebanese businessman operating in Lebanon, whether Arab or non-Arab, sooner or later fits into the pattern. If he fails to, he is weeded out.

An impelling process of identification takes place, the environment all the while shaping the alien into the image of the national businessman.

The process unfolds in many directions. However, this part of the inquiry did not aim at collecting information on all the interesting aspects of mobility of men and movement of ideas. Instead, it is limited to an investigation of certain components of the background of the business leader and of his mobility. The components include his national background, his religious affiliation, his father's occupation, his education and pre-entrepreneurial travel, the origins of entrepreneurial ideas, and changes in his career.

National Origin and Religion

Information on the citizenship and religious affiliation of the 207 business leaders is presented in summary form in Table D. Without drawing unwarranted conclusions about religion and enterprise, I feel that the information collected is interesting enough to justify a quick look at the cross-tabulation of religious affiliation with a number of other variables.

The most striking point in the distribution of respondents by religion is the wide discrepancy between this distribution and that of the whole population. Thus, though four fifths of the respondents are of the Christian faith, only half of the population is. On the other hand, the Moslems constitute about one sixth of the entrepreneurial group, but 44 per cent of the population. For the Druses, the discrepancy is even larger: 1.5 per cent of the respondents but 5.6 per cent of the population. Like the Christians, the Jews constitute a larger proportion of the business leaders (1.9 per cent) than of the population (0.4 per cent).

The association of religious affiliation with schooling shows that the Christian group is better educated than the Moslem group. The proportion of Moslem respondents is higher at the lower level of schooling, but lower at the higher level, than that of Christians.

A look at the religious distribution of business leaders by sector

Table D. Distribution of men in each sector by citizenship and by religion

Sector	*Total number*	*Original citizenship*	*Present citizenship*	*Religion*
Agriculture	16	16 Lebanese	16 Lebanese	10 Christians 6 Moslems
Industry	130	91 Lebanese 15 non-Lebanese Arabs 24 non-Arabs	118 Lebanese 5 non-Lebanese Arabs 7 non-Arabs	105 Christians 21 Moslems 3 Jews 1 Druse
Finance	14	7 Lebanese 6 non-Lebanese Arabs 1 non-Arab	11 Lebanese 2 non-Lebanese Arabs 1 non-Arab	11 Christians 2 Moslems 1 Jew
Services	47	35 Lebanese 10 non-Lebanese Arabs 2 non-Arabs	45 Lebanese 1 non-Lebanese Arab 1 non-Arab	40 Christians 5 Moslems 2 Druses
Totals	207	149 Lebanese 31 non-Lebanese Arabs[a] 27 non-Arabs[b]	190 Lebanese 8 non-Lebanese Arabs 9 non-Arabs	166 Christians 34 Moslems 4 Jews 3 Druses

[a] 15 Palestinians, 13 Syrians, 2 Iraqis, 1 Egyptian.
[b] 15 Armenians, 12 Europeans (French, Swiss, Polish, Czech).
Source: Data collected from the 207 questionnaires.

reveals the absence of Druse or Jewish respondents from agriculture. Moslems have a much larger share of the agriculture sector, and a slightly larger share of industry, than they have of finance and services. The Christians in Lebanon have a long historical lead over other communities in finance, trade, and services. Entrepreneurial tradition and institutions have been built around these sectors, and the necessary business contacts have been established for a long time. Indeed, there are indications that Moslem business leaders now have in industrial enterprise an outlet for their frustration at finding much of the opportunity in foreign trade, finance, and services already seized by their Christian counterparts.

Association between original nationality and form of organization indicates that the corporation is the most prevalent form used by respondents of Arab but non-Lebanese origin. This pattern can be satisfactorily explained. The Palestinians, who are the largest single component of this group, were already familiar with the corporate form of organization in Palestine. By contrast, out of fifteen establishments where the business leaders are Armenian, only two are incorporated. The difference is striking, considering that the two groups are equal in number and that both are refugee minorities operating in the same country under the same conditions. This is not merely a difference between an Arab and a non-Arab, since the thirteen Arab business leaders of Syrian origin have only three corporations among them and seem to prefer single ownership. Nor can it be a difference of religious affiliation, since all but two of the Palestinians are Christians, like all the Armenians and Syrians. So the explanation of the difference seems to lie mainly in the conditioning which the Palestinians had in Palestine and which neither the Armenians nor the Syrians ever had.

Armenian immigrants, furthermore, were severely short of capital funds on entering Lebanon after the First World War, and therefore had to launch out on a very modest scale, many of them single-handed. Those who prospered have on the whole preferred to remain the sole owners. Indeed, during the interviewing, several successful Armenian manufacturers were encountered who still tried to handle by themselves the functions of entrepreneur, manager, and foreman together, the way they had done in their humbler days. Their notions of organization seem to lag behind their technical views and experience.

Education and Travel

The illiterate entrepreneur who can hardly sign his name but who deals in millions of pounds generally makes sensational news but is not the prototype of entrepreneurs in Lebanon. Only 5 men

(2.4 per cent) were found who said they had had no formal schooling at all. There were 47 others (22.7 per cent) who failed to finish elementary school. On the other hand 119 men (57 per cent) completed high school, and 72 of those went on through college. Indeed, 34 of them continued further and received graduate or professional training. This distribution is out of line with that of the Lebanese population, in which the majority have had no more than elementary education, and the next largest segment are illiterate. Those educated in college and university are a small minority of the total population.

Men in the 30–39 age group are the most educated. They are a postwar crop of business leaders; most of them must have been in or approaching college when the war ended. The brief hesitation in enterprise during the war and just after, as well as the setting in of opulence, may have accounted for their long stay in school. In contrast, men now in their twenties who became business leaders in the 1950's may have been impatient to jump into the entrepreneurial fray during an extremely brisk business period. This may explain why in level of education they rank below men in the 30–39 age group. The data presented in Table E show that by far most of the respondents with high school, college, and graduate training started

Table E. Percentage distribution of men in each school group by date of entry into entrepreneurial ranks

	Entry into entrepreneurial ranks		
Years of schooling	*Before war*	*During war*	*After war*
None	100.0%	0.0%	0.0%
1–3	100.0	0.0	0.0
4–6	78.6	0.0	21.4
7–9	71.9	9.4	18.7
10–12	30.9	26.2	42.9
13–15	27.3	27.0	45.7
Over 15	42.5	3.0	54.5

Source: Table 289, which is listed in Appendix C.

their careers after the Second World War, and that most of the less-educated started before the war.

Although industrial activity is very technical, industry trails the other three sectors in the educational levels of its leaders: it is highest among the sectors in the proportion of its leaders having little or no schooling, and lowest in the proportion of its men having university education. Finance stands at the other extreme. This can be seen from Table F which gives the proportions of men at each

Table F. Percentage distribution of men in each sector by level of education

	Level of education			
Sector	*Subelementary and no schooling*	*Elementary*	*Secondary*	*University*
Agriculture	18.8%	6.3%	37.5%	37.5%
Industry	40.0	3.8	24.6	31.5
Finance	21.4	0.0	21.4	57.2
Services	36.1	2.1	12.8	48.9

Source: Table 329, which is listed in Appendix C.

level of education for each sector. A number of business leaders in industry (including most of the Armenians) have grown from the handicraft and workshop stage to the factory stage of manufacturing, or have come in with their attention focused more on the good prospects of industry than on their own qualifications. In many cases they stepped into manufacturing with an attitude and an outlook appropriate to commerce, and with very little specialized training. In this incongruity may lie the explanation of some of the contradictions in entrepreneurial behavior and choice.

Travel too is a form of education. More than 70 per cent of the business leaders (146 men) had traveled outside their country of origin before entering their present business career, and two thirds of this number had been abroad for more than one year. Business

Table G. Percentage distribution of men in each age group who had had pre-entrepreneurial travel, by duration of travel

Age group (years)	*Duration of travel*	
	One year or less	*Over one year*
20–29	53.8%	46.2%
30–39	28.1	71.9
40–49	18.2	81.8
50–59	14.3	85.7
60–69	14.3	85.7

Source: Table 140, which is listed in Appendix C.

ranked highest among the purposes of such travel, followed distantly by study and recreation. The older business leaders seem to have had greater travel experience than their younger colleagues, the amount of travel steadily increasing with age. The association of age and travel experience is shown in Table G.

The choice of sector by the respondents does not seem to have been noticeably influenced by their early travel experience. Indeed, most of the respondents themselves stated in reply to a direct question that their travel experience had not been a major factor in their choice of career. However, pre-entrepreneurial travel experience seems to have influenced the choice of the corporate form of ownership strongly, as can be seen from Table H. No less than 53 out of

Table H. Percentage distribution of men who had had pre-entrepreneurial travel, by form of ownership in establishment

	Duration of travel		
Form of ownership	(*1*) *One year or less*	(*2*) *Over one year*	(*3*) *Ratio of* (*2*) *to* (*1*)
Single ownership	34.5%	32.6%	0.96
Partnership	44.8	25.5	0.57
Corporation	20.7	41.9	2.02
Total	100.0	100.0	—

Source: Table 421, which is listed in Appendix C.

the total of 59 corporations are accounted for in the category of men with pre-entrepreneurial travel. In 41 cases out of the 53 the duration of travel had been over one year.

Fathers and Sons

The respondents were asked certain questions about the occupations and sources of income of their fathers. Although the answers of some of them may have deviated from the facts, either from lapses of memory or other reasons, the results in general warrant the inquiry.

The respondents, when asked for father's business or occupation, listed ten occupations. The most frequent was trade (31.3 per cent), followed by industry (26.4) and the professions (8.7). ("Industry" in this context ought to be understood as workshops and home industries—not heavily mechanized activity as the term is taken to mean in the present conditions of Lebanon.) Those three occupations account for two thirds of the fathers. The leading position of trade should be noted; we meet with it again when we come to discuss the business background of the respondents themselves.

In 97 cases, less than half of the total, father's occupation was traditional, in the sense that it ran back in the family; in fact 46 respondents said it ran back three generations or more. This phenomenon serves to point up the remarkable mobility between generations that comes out when we relate the fathers' occupations to the present sectors of their sons. In the following tabulation the respondents' present sectors are shown at the left, followed by the percentage distribution of the occupations of the fathers, as given by the respondents in their questionnaire answers.

Agriculture: trade, 30 per cent; industry, 15; landlordship, 15; agriculture, 10; other services, 10; other occupations, 20.

Industry: industry, 34 per cent; trade, 31; professions, 6; construction and real estate, 6; other occupations, 23.

Finance: trade, 44 per cent; professions, 25; agriculture, 6; finance, 6; landlordship, 6; other occupations, 13.

Services: trade, 29 per cent; industry, 16; professions, 12; government service, 7; agriculture, 7; other occupations, 29.

The most striking feature in this tabulation is that none of the sectors except industry has drawn the largest proportion of its entrepreneurs from the same background as that of the fathers. Agriculture, finance, and services have drawn most heavily on a background of trade.[7] Indeed, judging by these results, one must conclude that there is an avoidance of father's occupation in all sectors except industry.

Given this marked discrepancy between the generations, it is intriguing to find out why the sons are doing what they are. Investigation of the background of entrepreneurial ideas provides some of the answers. According to the data in hand, more of the respondents were led to their career by natural inclination to it than by anything else — that is, they felt an attraction to that career *in itself* apart from the attraction of profit prospects, the desire to follow father's business career, the pressure of urging by elders, the urge to contradict father, or the prestige expected in the career chosen.

Men in different age groups have been influenced in different degrees by natural inclination to the career chosen. Furthermore, wherever there has been high concentration of votes on natural inclination, there has been low concentration on pecuniary profit and on prestige as influences in choice of career, and vice versa. This pattern suggests a basic distinction between the force of profit and prestige on the one hand, and the force of natural inclination on the other hand. Men guided mainly by profit or prestige considerations seek a form of satisfaction that is externally discernible, whereas men guided mainly by natural inclination seek an inner satisfaction that does not press strongly for outward expression.

Admitted rebellions against fathers are few. Thus, the 207 respondents together made 326 choices of their reasons for entering their present career; yet only 3 of these choices were to avoid father's career or to contradict the urgings by elders. It is quite possible, however, that in many cases what seems like natural inclination may in fact also be a form of rebellion against the choice *expected* by elders.

The question of father-son relationship in the matter of choice of career was further pursued by asking the respondents what course in life their fathers most insistently wanted them to follow, and then by asking each respondent what he would rather his own son do. It was made clear to the respondents that the second question referred to the eldest son, if there was one, or to the nearest relative regarded as heir or heiress. The broad similarities between the two generations are striking. It appears that 42.5 per cent of the older generation wanted their sons to continue in the same career as themselves, 28.5 per cent allowed a free choice without interference, and 16.4 per cent wanted to see their sons take up a profession. All other desires are tiny by comparison. As for the present business leaders, 57.4 per cent of them would like to see their own sons continue in the same career as themselves, 10.7 per cent would allow a free choice, and 14.3 prefer a profession. Thus, the main differences are that the men of the second generation are more inclined to want their sons to follow in their footsteps, and the men of the older generation were more inclined to allow a free choice. Apparently the respondents rate their own businesses higher in the social and economic scale than their fathers before them.

The answers indicate that both generations think highly of the professions and both think little of government service or politics. The esteem in which the professions are held is general throughout the Arab world. But the low esteem of government service is quite atypical in that world. The high social status of business, and the affluence in which it basks in Lebanon, go a long way to explain why a business career is so much more desirable, and a government career so much less desirable, than in the neighboring Arab countries.

The valuation of careers varies with religious affiliation. All three respondents of the Druse faith and three of the four of the Jewish faith want their sons to keep family businesses going. On the other hand, 59 per cent of the Christians and only 44 per cent of the Moslems want such a continuation. This difference in attitude is more than one of valuation of business careers. It is also reflected in the divergent views of the two major religious groups on the value of professional careers. Thus 25 per cent of Moslem respondents but only 13 per cent of Christian respondents would like their sons to go into a professional career.

Equally significant differences emerge on comparison of the attitudes of the respondents with those of their fathers on the subject of business versus the professions. Here we see that only 41 per cent of the fathers of Christian respondents wanted a business career for their sons, as against 53 per cent of Moslem fathers. From one generation to the next, business has gained in attractiveness among the Christians (those favoring it increasing from 41 to 59 per cent) but has declined among the Moslems (53 to 44 per cent). The reverse is true in connection with the professions, which seemed attractive to 16 per cent of the Christian and 15 per cent of the Moslem fathers, whereas among the sons the figure dropped to 13 per cent of the Christians and rose to 25 per cent of the Moslems. In brief, attitudes to business and to professions vary no less from one generation to another than between one religious group and another.

Change of Career

Information on the mobility of the entrepreneurs leads to two main findings. The first is that 53 per cent of the total came to assume the authority they now have without having worked previously in any business firm. Nine of these men (including four priests) had been in the professions, and seven in government service. One man had been a *rentier*. The rest had moved into an entrepreneurial career right after school. Furthermore, the more recently men have made their entry, the less often have they come from a background of business. Why is this? One tentative explanation is that as we get closer to the present we find that schooling extends longer and reaches higher levels. It is very likely that this lengthening creates an impatience among potential entrepreneurs and an eagerness to start an independent business career without further delay.

The second finding is that by far the largest single group of respondents—almost half of those who had been in business before assuming entrepreneurial authority—came from trade. As in the case of their fathers, the two most important business careers in the personal background of the respondents were trade and industry; they account for about two thirds of the cases.[8]

In this general setting trade plays an important role as a reservoir of entrepreneurial talent, since it is the largest single source of entrepreneurs. Thus, although trading activity may not itself be remarkably innovational, or, if innovational, then of dubious *direct* value for development, it is still of great value in conditioning potential entrepreneurs for the special activity which awaits them. It familiarizes businessmen with the special characteristics of foreign products and possibly with production processes. It also tends to increase sensitivity to markets and prices, and to sharpen awareness of opportunities. But to say this is not to say that a background in trade is an unmixed blessing. Our later examination of the quality of enterprise in Lebanon will suggest that it is not.

The business leaders who had changed careers admitted several reasons for the change. They were refreshingly frank in assigning the greatest weight to the expectation of larger profit in the new career. Second place was assigned to the expectation of greater security and "future." It is true that the question on the motivation of change was put to many of the respondents years after the actual shift. It can only be assumed that in replying they tried to be honest; yet unconsciously some respondents may have rationalized a move now distant in their past. They may have described the motives which during the interview seemed to them to be paramount in *any* move. Nevertheless, the answers are revealing.

In relating the motives to the sectors, we notice that men moving into industry have been motivated mostly by the desire for greater security and a "better future," as well as for prestige. This is not surprising: trade, finance, and services are activities where, generally speaking, the most lucrative opportunities are already seized by people well established in the field. Furthermore, the entrepreneurial newcomers are building their own system of prestige-rating; they feel that slowly they are inheriting the glamour that trade has so far had. The relative strength of each of the motives for men in each of the sectors can be seen in Table I.

Table I. Percentage distribution of men in each sector by reasons given for change from previous into present career[a]

	Reasons for change						
Sector	*Profit*	*Prestige*	*Power*	*Security*	*Acquaintance*	*Other*	*No answer*
Agriculture	16.67%	0.00%	0.00%	16.67%	16.67%	50.00%	0.00%
Industry	23.96	12.50	4.17	27.08	5.21	27.08	0.00
Finance	22.22	11.11	11.11	0.00	0.00	55.56	0.00
Services	29.27	9.76	2.44	14.63	2.44	39.02	2.44

[a] Percentages add horizontally to 100.
Source: Table 364, which is listed in Appendix C.

Trade is decreasing not only in glamour but also in power. The merchant community is still very influential socially and politically, but a great deal of its power is unmistakably passing to financial tycoons. From a focal position of strategy in finance, they are reaching into industry, housing development, transport. Man for man, the banking sector is possibly more powerful today than any other sector. Conversely, the services sector has few of these nonpecuniary attractions.

Agriculture is a case by itself. The appeal of this sector to those who have moved into it is divided equally among profit, security, and better acquaintance with the activity involved. The last factor has a pull in agriculture which is overwhelmingly stronger than in any other sector, or for that matter than any other pull operating on any of the sectors. This finding ties in well with the fact that more of those today in agriculture than in any other sector came from the landlord class.

Three final observations can be made on the subject of change of career. First, the power of the profit motive, as of the security motive, was given more weight by Moslem respondents than by Christians. Second, the profit motive was given more weight by single men than by married men, and the factor of security more weight by the married than by the single. Third, the profit motive is higher among married respondents who have no children than among those who have children, and the desire for security is higher among those with children. None of these findings comes as a surprise.

Movement by business leaders into their present careers seems for most of them to be the end of journeying from sector to sector. Less than one fifth plan to leave their present major field of activity, and three fourths of those who plan to leave expect to keep a foot in their present sector or subsector, though turning most of their attention elsewhere. This information indicates a large measure of stability in the sectoral distribution of the present community of business leaders, and probably a high level of satisfaction with the career chosen, or at least a low level of dissatisfaction with it.

The intention to make a shift in career grows smaller as the respondents grow older, except for those in their sixties, who seem more interested in making a shift than men in their fifties. Can it be that men who are very close to the age of retirement entertain ideas which give them the satisfaction that they are still active and dynamic? On this speculative note the matter will be allowed to rest.

A clear picture emerges when plans for a shift in career are related to marital status and to the presence of children. There is a reluctance among the married to make a new move, whereas many of the single, no doubt feeling a greater degree of freedom of action, declared their intention to do so. Among the married, more men with children plan to make a new move than men without children. It is clear that concern for his dependents outweighs the married man's desire for stability.

Respondents who intend to leave their present business want to strike out in many directions, but with a concentration (46.5 per cent) on industry, especially among the young. Second place is occupied by trade (19 per cent), third place by finance (12.7 per cent), and fourth place by agriculture (9.5 per cent). It is quite revealing of the scale of values that services are relegated to fifth place along with several other destinations.

But those who want to change career, it will be recalled, are a small minority among the business leaders. The majority expressed contentment in their careers plus a determination to improve their businesses and thus satisfy any lingering urge for change that they may have. Further evidence of contentment came when the business leaders were asked what they would do if they had their lives to live again. Almost three fourths of them said they would choose the same career. However, contentment seemed to drop slightly as the age of respondents rose.

Mobility can involve not only entry into but exit from business. Only in rare cases do entrepreneurs move out into a government job or a Bohemian existence. A bankrupt entrepreneur can occasionally be found as a clerk or salesman in somebody else's shop. But in the majority of cases, exit means either death while at the job, or retirement at an advanced age.

Retirement is a matter of special interest in a study of enterprise; it is closely connected to "turnover" in a country's reservoir of entrepreneurial resources. The retirement habits of a business community determine to a large extent the entry of new blood into business, which is one way of rejuvenating entrepreneurship.

The respondents were asked about their intentions concerning retirement and handing over responsibility, and their plans for activities after retirement. These questions seemed to have more than a touch of the unreal to the respondents, most of whom were far from the usual retirement age. Many of those who were willing to answer gave the impression that they were treating the subject lightly, or else in a totally abstract way as though it did not relate to them. Notwithstanding this impression, the replies will be reported and discussed.

A little under one third of the respondents, when asked if they planned to retire from business "at some future date," said they did. None of these was in the 20–29 age group; likewise the only man over 70 had no intention of retiring. The proportion of men with such intention in the intervening age groups tended to get smaller as the age of respondents rose. It is quite possible that, in the face of the inevitability of his aging, man stubbornly convinces himself that he is too strong and active to consider bowing out. There is, of course, a more charitable possible explanation—the attachment men acquire for their career the longer they stay with it. The two theses are not contradictory but in fact supplement each other.

Not all of the 70 men who said they intended to retire had the same deadline in mind. Fourteen of them, in fact, said they planned to retire at 50 or younger; 21 aimed at retiring between age 51 and 60; and 20 others between 61 and 70. Two men said 71 or older, and the remaining 13 gave no target date.

Married respondents were slightly more intent on retiring than unmarried respondents. Furthermore, there was a substantially larger proportion intending to retire among the married with children than among the childless. The plans of the business leader seem to be influenced by the question of succession, which is, in turn, quite relevant to the form of business ownership. Thus, the largest proportion of men planning to retire were in singly owned establishments, the lowest in partnerships. The fact that a man in a single ownership is confident of being succeeded by his heir probably makes him less reluctant to consider retirement and the handing over of responsibility than his colleague in a partnership or a corporation who cannot feel equally confident.

The largest category of respondents intending to retire favored traveling as a pastime. The next largest group frankly admitted a desire to do nothing—just to relax. For a third group, the life of a gentleman-farmer had a special appeal. The smallest group stated that they would stand by to give advice to their successors if asked to. Retired businessmen in other countries make very much the same choices.

THE MAINSPRING OF INNOVATION*

What are the sources of entrepreneurial ideas? How do business leaders attempt to keep the flow of innovational ideas into business reasonably strong? These two questions are near the heart of any inquiry into the adequacy of entrepreneurial resources in a developing economy.

The Sources of Ideas

The business leaders were asked, "How did you get the idea of establishing (or acquiring or entering) your present business (or, if you are a salaried executive or merely a shareholder, of taking over entrepreneurial responsibility)?" They were given seven specific sources of entrepreneurial ideas, along with the opportunity of specifying others, and were requested to rank their answers if they gave more than one.

The largest concentration of "votes" regardless of ranking went to the business leader's "own interest or initiative or inventiveness" (26 per cent), followed by "accident" (17 per cent), "contacts with other businessmen" (16 per cent), "training and experience" (9 per cent), "influence of a close relative" (8 per cent), "traveling" (7 per cent), and "education" (6 per cent).

Ranked according to their rating as first, second, third, or fourth choice, these sources take a somewhat different significance. First *and* second place were occupied by the business leader's "own interest or initiative or inventiveness" (followed in each case by contacts with other businessmen). Traveling got third place and training fourth place. But whereas all 207 respondents made a first choice, the number dropped to 108 for a second choice, to 32 for a third choice, and down to 7 for a fourth choice. The heavy concentration of votes on the first and second choices indicates the overwhelming emphasis the respondents place on the mainspring within themselves. If indeed the entrepreneur's own interest and

* The findings in this section are based on Tables 45, 60–63, 122–125, 156–159, 170–172, 222–224, 259, 260, 294–298, 321, 322, 365, 413. See Appendix C for list of Tables 1 through 472 and explanation of where they may be found.

initiative supplied the idea of the business — as the answers indicate — the entrepreneurial resources of Lebanon are probably capable of generating their own innovational drive and of keeping it alive and active.

The relation of those answers to the respondent's age, sector, and school level yields the following observations.

1) The older the business leader, the greater the emphasis he places on his interest and initiative, and the less on accident. The trend is consistent all through the age structure.

2) The consistency should, however, be viewed with some skepticism. Probably the position which the business leaders take is more a function of their self-confidence *at the time of interviewing* than of their feeling when they actually started their career. The younger business leaders, being closer to the start of their career, and not having accumulated a great deal of experience and confidence, are likely to show more humility.

3) The very young business leaders attribute a great deal to the influence of close relatives and to "accident" (such as inheriting the business). Their fathers are probably more enlightened and sophisticated — and therefore more influential in shaping their sons' careers — than were the fathers of the older business leaders.

4) Education is credited with very little influence as a source of entrepreneurial ideas, and the influence does not seem to grow as the level of education rises. Underlying this phenomenon, perhaps, is the businessman's contempt for what he terms "academic" education as a valuable asset for business success.

Rejuvenation of the Entrepreneurial Spirit

The fountain of innovation is fuller than ever before for the underdeveloped country that wants to draw on it. The experience of the developed world is an open book to be copied; the goods and services as well as the methods of production and organization of this world are within the reach of those who are willing to introduce new business ideas into traditional economies. This accessibility of advanced technology has become possible through the exposure of developed countries to the gaze of large portions of the underdeveloped world.

Acquaintance by men from underdeveloped countries with advanced technology can come in many ways. One major way is education and training obtained by these men in developed countries, or at home in institutions established by organizations from developed countries, or in domestic institutions under teachers trained abroad. Travel abroad in developed countries is also a great eye-opener. Fairs and exhibitions, technical journals and books, are important carriers of information from areas of advanced to areas of backward technology. Foreign entrepreneurs who are allowed entry into underdeveloped countries can bring in innovational ideas.

Lebanon has benefited from all these forms of exposure to advanced technology. A business leader in Lebanon, even more than his counterparts in most other underdeveloped countries, has no excuse to let his entrepreneurial faculties go sterile — and the record indicates that he has not let this happen. The high educational standards of business leaders in Lebanon and their wide travel experience have already been reported. In addition, over nine tenths of the respondents stated that they buy technical literature for themselves and their staff, both in Arabic and in foreign languages. About seven tenths visit fairs, mostly but by no means exclusively in the Arab world. Generally speaking, the higher the level of education of respondents, and the younger they are, the less frequently do they visit fairs.

Fresh innovational ideas from the outside world can be implemented as true copies of what has been learned; they can also stir local entrepreneurial talent into some creativeness and adaptation in the process of adoption. It need hardly be emphasized that it would be unrealistic to expect the business leaders in Lebanon to make primary innovations.

These men are aware of their possibilities and of their limitations. In the investigation we attempted to find out their attitude toward developing new products or methods through the adaptation of advanced products or methods, and the degree of their faith in their ability to do so. On the question of products, almost seven tenths of them said they do not attempt to influence public tastes but, by and large, to catch up with changes already occurring in the market. This is truest of respondents between 30 and 60 years of age. It is also truest of men in agriculture. On the other hand, almost nine tenths of the respondents stated that they try to evolve new methods or processes within their establishment — an affirmation clearly in contradiction with their avowed timidity in facing the market. It is indeed puzzling that a group of men that seem so active in trying to innovate in their production and organization should declare themselves largely nonaggressive in their sales policies and practices. This could make sense only in a market where producers enjoy a high degree of security from competition, or in a situation of blissful ignorance of the potency of advertising as a promoter of sales. In Lebanon the explanation may lie more in ignorance than in security. It may also betray an overestimation of the power to evolve new methods and processes.

The role which "new blood" plays in the introduction of new products and methods is of major importance. This new blood need not have foreign origins. Domestic technicians, for example, whether in the employ of the establishment or not, are eager to put their training and experience into use. The readiness with which business leaders admit technicians into their councils determines in some part the degree to which entrepreneurial ideas are kept flowing into the economy.

The inquiry was not designed to gauge directly the extent to which the talent of technicians was being welcomed into the higher echelons of entrepreneurial authority. Nevertheless the impression was gained from the interviews that the business leaders are opening the door to this talent only cautiously. This impression is strengthened by the finding, reported earlier, of the opposition of most business leaders to the delegation of entrepreneurial authority to senior staff. The question of the entry of "new blood" into business is related to that of the retirement of business leaders and the opportunity this creates for younger men to take over. The attitude of these leaders to retirement has been reported; we need add nothing to that point here except to state that the well-trained technicians aspiring to entrepreneurial rank meet most resistance when they are not kin to the business leaders. Under the circumstances, a technician who has business drive will find much more scope for his ambitions in a brand-new establishment where he starts by being top man.

As for the entry into Lebanon of foreign entrepreneurs, a high degree of tolerance of this flow of talent is evident. Almost three fourths of the respondents are in favor of entry, with men in the 60–69 and 20–29 age groups well in the lead. Men in agriculture and in services tend to favor the foreign entrepreneur more than men in finance and industry. Industrialists, being in the newest and least familiar field of activity, apparently feel least secure. Financiers, working in an efficient and already vastly expanded sector, seem to be unenthusiastic over the entry of foreign bankers. The irony of the situation is that foreigners are likely to want to enter the very sectors where they are least welcome.

The more educated the business leaders, the greater their willingness to allow foreigners to come and set up business. This welcoming attitude was more obvious among Christian than Moslem respondents. Since the level of education of Christians is on the whole higher than that of Moslems, the two factors of religious affiliation and education supplement each other. Christians, while on the whole more welcoming than their Moslem colleagues, were behind the Moslems in welcoming business leaders from Arab countries. Otherwise, regardless of religion, the respondents who favored entry showed little preference on grounds of nationality.

The conditions on which the respondents favored the entry of non-Lebanese business leaders were not often severe; indeed, some 14 per cent of the replies included no conditions at all. The condition that the newcomers should set up new enterprises was emphasized most frequently (30 per cent). Next came the condition that control of new enterprises should remain in Lebanese hands through Lebanese ownership of a major share of capital. Lastly came the condition that newcomers should bring capital as well as new ideas.

THE QUALITY OF ENTERPRISE*

The business leaders of Lebanon will not be classified into types here, although there is a strong case in a book like this one for devoting some space to a discussion of entrepreneurial types. Instead, the quality of enterprise will be examined for characteristics that usually underlie classificatory systems. This may be the appropriate way of dealing with types in a real situation where entrepreneurial resources are in a state of flux, as they are in Lebanon.

The quality of enterprise will be ascertained through the attitudes of business leaders in four areas of behavior. The first area is the use of professional services and practices that enable the establishment to approach problems and decisions rationally—through calculation and scientific research, rather than by rule of thumb.[9] The second is the area of decision-making and the approaches to it; the third that of daring and aggressiveness in innovation; and the fourth area that of investment, turnover, and time preferences.

Professional Services and Practices

Most of the professional services and practices at the disposal of the business leader in advanced countries have their counterparts in Lebanon, though certainly not at the same level of development. The ones singled out for examination in interviews were not complex and sophisticated, for the results would be misleading if the professional services characterizing a highly developed economy were chosen.

The inquiry centered around three practices. It developed that double-entry bookkeeping is used by 97 per cent of the respondents,

* The findings in this section are based on Tables 67–83, 86, 87, 94, 98, 109, 114, 179–186, 189–192, 199, 203, 212, 233, 243, 263, 265, 301–306, 369–373, 378–380, 396, 405, 436–446, 459. See Appendix C for list of Tables 1 through 472 and explanation of where they may be found.

but that cost accounting is used by only 60 per cent, and external audit services by only 54 per cent. There are several reasons why almost half the business leaders avoid the use of external audit services. First of all, there is no law in Lebanon that sets standards for audit: any accountant can put up a sign as auditor. This generally makes the auditor less of a strict independent inspector and more of a hired professional man eager to please his employer. But this is by no means the only reason for avoidance. There is also the fear that an external auditor may produce a profit and loss statement that will cost the establishment more than it cares to pay in taxes. And there is simple ignorance of the value of having accounts examined by competent auditors (of whom there are a few), coupled with the belief that an internal audit is sufficient for all practical purposes.

Younger respondents comprised a higher proportion than older respondents, and better-educated than less-educated respondents, of men who declared that they use the three practices. This pattern is truer of corporations than of single ownerships or of partnerships. As for the sectors, men in the services-producing sectors (finance and services) surpassed those in the commodity-producing sectors (agriculture and industry) in the use of double-entry bookkeeping and external audit—but in cost accounting it was the other way around. (See Table J for the association between the use of professional services and practices, on the one hand, and, on the other hand, the age and schooling of respondents and the sector and form of ownership of their establishments.)

Attitudes toward research and insurance were treated as additional indications of sophisticated enterprise. The majority of business leaders stated their belief in the value of research institutions and their readiness to pay them to conduct studies. Nevertheless, only a small number of these men had in fact sought the assistance of research organizations. We believe the blame should be shared by the business leaders and by the organizations, which have failed to make businessmen realize fully the usefulness of research to business. Life insurance and other types of personal insurance,

Table J. Percentage of men in each age group, school group, sector, and form of ownership who use double-entry bookkeeping, cost accounting, and external audit

	Double-entry bookkeeping	*Cost accounting*	*External audit*
AGE GROUP (YEARS)			
20–29	100.0%	63.3%	75.0%
30–39	100.0	71.7	58.5
40–49	96.5	68.4	56.1
50–59	95.2	55.5	44.4
60–69	88.2	29.4	50.9
70 and over	100.0	0.0	0.0
SCHOOLING (YEARS)			
None	80.0	20.0	20.0
1–3	100.0	0.0	0.0
4–6	92.9	64.3	42.9
7–9	96.9	40.6	40.6
10–12	97.7	65.9	56.8
13–15	97.4	68.4	68.4
Over 15	97.1	76.5	70.6
SECTOR			
Agriculture	81.3	50.0	6.3
Industry	96.9	66.2	54.6
Finance	100.0	14.3	64.3
Services	100.0	65.9	65.9
FORM OF OWNERSHIP			
Single ownership	94.1	52.9	35.3
Partnership	97.5	66.3	46.3
Corporation	98.3	64.4	86.4

Source: Tables 180–182, 302–304, 371–373, and 438–440, which are listed in Appendix C.

though growing in popularity, are still not very common: less than half of the business leaders carry personal insurance. The others believe that their business is their best insurance, or that the premiums to be paid can be more lucratively used elsewhere. A smaller proportion of the very young and the very old carry personal insurance than of men in the middle age groups. Not surprisingly, single men are less interested than married men, especially those with children.

There is also a marked difference in attitude between the two major religious groups. Almost twice as large a proportion of Christians as of Moslems carry personal insurance. Whereas members of both faiths believe that the life of man is in the hands of God, the Moslems seem to carry their belief to its logical conclusion and to place more trust in God's will. This is especially true of the traditional, practicing Moslems.*

The Road to Decision-making

Decision-making is the essence of entrepreneurial authority. In defining the entrepreneur earlier in this study we stated that decision-making with regard to issues involving innovation was the key to the locus of the entrepreneurial function. A study of the quality of enterprise could be made exclusively from an analysis of the decisions made by entrepreneurs — but nothing so ambitious is attempted here. Instead, a few issues relevant to decision-making will be examined.

Consultation versus a closed process of decision. One issue is that of consultation. The alternative favored by the largest number of respondents was consultation with external experts. Next came consultation with subordinates, followed by no consultation — that is, independent decision-making. About three fourths of the business leaders voted for one of these three alternatives, thereby excluding the reference of business matters to the judgment of relatives or friends who do not belong to the establishment. In other words, there is here a clear dissociation of business matters from the realm of personal relations. The choice that seems to appeal

* The respondents were also asked whether the business was at all insured and, if so, against what risks. It turned out that certain types of business insurance are mandatory by Lebanese law. As the design of the question had not taken this fact into account, the answers lost their significance as indicators of the quality of enterprise. Consequently the findings are not reported here.

least is the consultation with friends and relatives who are outside the establishment.

The answers, as can be seen from Table K, show that independent decision-making appeals most to manufacturers and least to

Table K. Percentage distribution of men in each sector and school group by attitude toward consultation in the process of decision-making[a]

	Independent decision (no consultation)	*Consult friends*	*Consult subordinates*	*Consult friends and subordinates*	*Consult experts*	*Other*
SECTOR						
Agriculture	14.8%	7.4%	18.5%	18.5%	40.7%	0.0%
Industry	19.4	4.3	23.1	14.5	31.2	7.5
Finance	13.6	9.1	22.7	18.2	36.4	0.0
Services	17.4	2.9	23.2	20.3	33.3	2.9
SCHOOLING (YEARS)						
None	83.3	0.0	0.0	0.0	16.7	0.0
1–3	0.0	0.0	50.0	0.0	50.0	0.0
4–6	50.0	0.0	6.3	18.7	25.0	0.0
7–9	15.9	2.3	29.5	13.6	31.8	6.8
10–12	15.6	4.7	17.2	18.7	35.9	7.8
13–15	15.3	3.4	23.7	22.0	33.9	1.7
Over 15	16.4	5.5	21.8	12.7	34.5	9.0

[a] Percentages add horizontally to 100, but, because of rounding, not always exactly.
Source: Tables 300 and 369, which are listed in Appendix C.

financiers. The financiers put more weight on consultation, and are better disposed than the other sectors toward the advice of nonbusiness friends. The attitude of manufacturers may seem strange, in view of the obvious need for outside technical advice. In explanation, it can be contended that the more innovational the activity, the greater the degree of aggressiveness in enterprise, and that the more aggressive the entrepreneur the greater his tendency to act independently. Hence the position of manufacturers. On the other hand, the nature of financial deals and the extreme secretiveness they require justify notable reliance by financiers on the opinion of trusted friends and relatives outside the business, while the large size of such deals necessitates the caution manifest in the low level of independent action.

Cross-tabulated with the form of business organization, the answers reveal a much smaller extent of independent action in the corporation than in the single ownership or the partnership. Subordinates are consulted more in the corporation. Men in partnerships had the lowest level of consultation with subordinates and the highest preference for independent action. The fact that these men have partners poses no contradiction with their claim that they act independently. In most partnerships encountered there was a large measure of division of authority in the establishment, enabling each partner to act independently on a wide range of matters.

Calculation or inspiration? A supplementary question was posed: Do the respondents, in making major decisions, rely more on thorough calculation and statistical evidence or on their own perception and their "feel" of a situation? A little more than half the respondents, mostly men below 40, stated that theirs was the course of calculation and evidence. The rest, mostly men above 40, indicated the second way. Both groups were clear in their minds where they stood. Those relying more on calculation took the position that their perception guides them among the many possibilities and opportunities their business presents, but that it is down-to-earth calculation and factual evidence that helps them finally make up their mind one way or another. Those others who rely more on their own perception contend that they do some calculation in the initial stages of examination of an issue, but that in the end it is their perception that moves them in the direction of a decision. Thus, in the end, the difference was mainly one of emphasis.

Industry and finance stood at the two extremes, with manufacturers heavily in favor of calculation and financiers of perception.

Here again, as in a few other cases, men in finance reveal a traditionalist attitude and approach in line with the view they hold that their activity is noninnovational and to that extent not exacting in its use of the trimmings of sophisticated enterprise.

Strangely enough, the level of education does not appear to be influential in the shaping of positions taken by respondents. This might mean that, although with more years of schooling business leaders accept professional services readily, they do so without conscious commitment in their style of decision-making. They can use professional services and still feel that the major decisions are made through a sixth sense.

There is a clear-cut association between the answers on style of decision-making and the form of business organization. Calculativeness looms larger in partnerships than in single ownerships, and in corporations largest of all. On several previous occasions strong association appeared between rational enterprise and the choice of the corporation (or even the partnership) as a form of business organization. The issue of calculation provides one more piece of evidence of this association.

The desired image of associates. In order to throw light on what sort of men the respondents would like to have as their senior associates, they were given a list of ten qualities and asked to indicate the qualities that appeal most to them. The qualities that obtained more than 10 per cent of the vote are those of direct relevance to the operation of the establishment—that is, honesty, technical efficiency, ability to get along with people, hard work, and self-reliance. The qualities that received less support were ones that do not seem especially to endear the executive to the entrepreneur or do not seem to matter much for the business either way in the entrepreneur's opinion.

Perhaps it can be said on these grounds that the entrepreneurial resources of Lebanon have broken out of the cast of rigid, traditional attitudes and behavior patterns of less enterprising communities. However, not a single clear or significant pattern emerges on examination of the opinions of respondents in conjunction with their age, their education, their sector, or the form of organization of their establishments.

Only the attitudes of the two major religious groups differ noticeably. True, Christians and Moslems were about even in their regard for honesty as a quality in their business associates. Among the characteristics to which the Christians attached more importance than did the Moslems were "shrewdness, even if they are not very honest"; "ability to get along well with people"; "influence in government circles"; and "not being a close relative." Among the characteristics to which the Moslems attached more importance than did the Christians were "hard work"; "technical efficiency in your line of business"; and "being a close relative of yours." It is clear that a greater degree of sophistication and self-confidence appears in the Christians' patterns of choice. The Moslems, on the other hand, emphasize the straightforward, solid qualities of hard work and efficiency and show an old-fashioned preference for relatives.

Gregariousness and competitiveness. The inclination toward gregariousness or competitiveness throws further light on the quality of enterprise. When the business leaders were asked whether they associate with other businessmen who have the same interest — in pressing government to follow (or parliament to legislate) certain policies appropriate to their business — 63 per cent of them answered in the affirmative. The inclination to associate rises slightly as age rises.

However, from investigation beyond the actual interviewing and beyond the four sectors included in this study, the fact emerged that there is little association and cooperation among businessmen in other areas of action, even when there is promise of high rewards for the industry and for the establishments within it. This fragmentation is carried to the absurd point at which definite damage is suffered by groups and individuals because of lack of cooperation. The most conspicuous instance is in the fruit export industry where a lucrative line of business is being damaged owing to the absence of common standards of grading, standardized packing, and uniform pricing. There is little long-term rationality in the business leader's attitude, and it is doubtful that he makes substantial gains from his atomistic approach except in the very short run.

Related to the issue of association is the policy favored by the business leader toward competitors. This policy can be one of *collusion,* where he comes to terms with them with regard to operations; one of *peaceful coexistence,* under which he ignores them in the conviction that there is room for him as well as for them; or one of *eviction,* under which he tries to force them out. If he tries eviction, he may aim at achieving this by buying out, underselling, developing better distribution services, improving quality of products and services, or reducing costs. Obviously he may adopt a combination of policies.

Asked which of the three policies they favored for dealing with competitors, the largest single group of the respondents (46 per cent) chose eviction. And most of that group preferred to achieve this end through improving the quality of product. The policy ranking second was that of collusion; the third place was occupied by the policy of ignoring competitors on the principle that the market is large enough for all.

Faith in measures to force competitors out tends to grow weaker as the observer moves from the lower to the higher age groups. On the other hand, as age rises the tendency grows stronger to favor collusion or indifference. One might infer from these results that "wisdom" creeps in as age increases.

If this wisdom is mixed with cynicism, it nonetheless reveals a realistic appraisal of the possible as distinct from the preferable. To come to terms with competitors on operations, or even to ignore them, or to hope to capture their market by reducing one's own costs, seems to appeal to the business leader more strongly as he grows older than does capturing that market by underselling, by improvement in quality and method of distribution, or by outright purchase of the competing business. The bankers showed more of this realism than the others, probably realizing how costly and impractical it would be for them to force competitors out of the market and how sensible collusion or indifference must be. On the other hand, in both industry and services, where the market is atomistic, eviction of competitors won a larger vote than other policies. The difference in attitude is the joint product of differences in circumstances and in temperament. The basic personality difference is likely at an early stage to move one businessman in the direction of industry and another in the direction of finance, and later on to characterize the approach of each to the problem of competition. But temperament is probably less influential than circumstance in the selection of policy toward competitors. The structure of each of the sectors with regard to the number and force of the competing units is probably more of a determining factor in the attitude of a business leader than his innate preference.

Daring and Aggressiveness in Innovation

Some further insight into the quality of enterprise may be gained from an examination of certain decisions that business leaders take or believe they will take in the face of changing conditions.

Superior products, superior methods, and the willingness to change. The respondent was first asked how his establishment would be affected by the readiness of the market for a new product that is a substitute for the one he produces, one that is seemingly a more promising product. It was suggested to the respondent that he could: shift as soon as possible to the new product regardless of the risk involved; wait until the new product proves its profitability before making a decision; undersell competitors or otherwise weaken the prospects of the new product; or take some other attitude.

Each of the first two courses — shifting immediately, and waiting it out — drew some 31 per cent of the replies; the third course — fighting back — drew about 11 per cent. The youngest group of business leaders seem to be the most cautious in their reaction. Taking all age groups and the three main alternatives into account, we find a slight tendency for the desire for a speedy shift to rise as age rises, and, conversely, for the desire to wait to drop as age rises. Men in the services-producing sectors and men in corporations were considerably more pronounced in their preference for a shift to promising new products than men in the commodity-producing sectors and in single ownerships or partnerships. Men in industry and agriculture must have considered their physical plant a factor for rigidity and viewed their inputs as more "specific" than inputs in finance and services.

The respondent was also asked how his establishment would be affected by the development of a new process (or machine) that is technically superior to the one he is currently using. This question produced a much stronger reaction. More than four fifths of the respondents declared themselves in favor of a speedy shift or of a search for a process superior to the new one that threatens the process in existence. This enthusiasm contrasts sharply with the hesitation concerning the shift to new, superior products. As several respondents stated, new products are appearing all the time, and it would be wasteful, if not hopeless, to try to keep up with the flow. But adoption of new machines or new processes is a sensible policy. Such innovations do not appear as fast as new products, and in any case they had better be adopted if the establishment is to face the resulting challenge to its products.

The answers concerning a new process, like those concerning a new product, indicate that men in finance and in services are ahead of men in agriculture and industry in their willingness to shift speedily. And the reasons for this difference in attitude are most probably the same as in the case of shift to new products. Likewise, the corporation again leads in the desire for change.

Prosperity, depression, and entrepreneurial qualities. No matter what explanation of the business cycle is put forth by the economic theorist or historian, the businessman remains the central actor around whose action or inaction the explanation largely moves. His atomistic decisions are of primary significance for the level and directions of general economic activity in the community. Hence our interest in the reactions of business leaders to prosperity and to depression.

The most popular reaction to prosperity was expansion within the establishment, both in sales and in capital and outfit, and the least popular was restriction of sales for the purpose of reaping high returns per unit sold.

Three patterns emerge from the inquiry regarding prosperity. The first portrays the attitude of a minority who indicated the desire not to expand the volume of business, or to expand it only slightly in order to obtain a rise in the margin of profit per unit of sales. This is an illustration of shortsightedness and irrational acquisitiveness. The second pattern portrays the attitude of those who indicated a preference for expansion in volume of sales and a drop in the margin of profit per unit sold. The third pattern describes the attitudes of those who emphasized expansion in outfit. The second and third patterns reveal expansionism — the one characterized by rational acquisitiveness and market-consciousness, the other by the same features and, in addition, by investment-consciousness.

This classification fits the respondents regardless of sector or age. However, the clearest and most consistent pattern emerges from the examination of reactions in relation to forms of business organization. Irrational, short-sighted acquisitiveness characterizes the single ownership, and to a lesser extent the partnership. Conversely, rational market-consciousness as well as investment-consciousness characterize the corporation.

Further evidence of the predominantly farsighted and expansive attitude of the respondents came out when they were asked about their reaction to depression. Only 30 per cent of them said they would contract their operations, while 64 per cent said they would keep the same volume of operations. More than half of this larger group indicated their readiness to accept a much lower price and profit rather than contract operations; a little less than half said they would even accept an outright loss, so long as they could stand it, rather than contract.

This asserted tenacity derives from four main sources, according to the interview results. The predominant one is the expectation of improvement in business conditions. The second is concern over the difficulty of recruiting new staff and laborers to replace the ones who have to be laid off in case of contraction. The third is the high cost of termination and compensation allowance to laid-off employees under Lebanese laws, at a time when business can ill afford such cost. And the fourth is concern for the prestige of the establishment and its leaders in case of contraction. As the interviewing took place after a six-month political upheaval in Lebanon during which economic activity dropped considerably, the respondents drew on their recent experience in their answers.

"Normal profit" and critical profit. Another test applied in order to assess the tenacity of business leaders in the face of hardship was to find out what they thought their reaction would be if their returns dropped below certain minimally desirable limits. This inquiry involves the concept of "normal profit"—a rate of profit, or a range of rates, which the businessman considers adequate for his investment. The range of normal profit that drew the largest concentration of votes was 10–12 per cent per annum on investment. One fourth of the respondents chose this range, which also comprised the median around which the respondents were divided. About 15 per cent of them wanted something above 22 per cent.

Those who said they would not pull out of business if their profit fell below the "normal profit" were further asked at what point, if at all, they would pull out and what they would take into consideration in making up their minds. Thus, what seems most significant is not the level of the range of profit stated as adequate, nor the lower rate deemed critical for staying or for pulling out, but the size of the gap between the normal-profit range and the lower rate, together with the factors that would be taken into account before the crucial decision to pull out was taken. Table L, con-

Table L. Distribution of men with respect to attitude if profit dropped below range considered adequate by them

Attitude that would be taken	*Number of men*	*Per cent of total*
Would withdraw only if there were outright losses, sustained and with no hope of improvement	84	40.6
Would withdraw if profits dropped to a positive figure well below the lower end of the range of adequate profit	63	30.4
Would withdraw only if profits dropped to zero	31	15.0
Would withdraw as soon as profits dropped below the lower end of the range of adequate profit	11	5.3
No reply	18	8.7
Total	207	100.0

Source: Data directly collected from the 207 questionnaires.

structed from answers to several questions in the questionnaires, presents the position of all 207 respondents.

Predominantly, the entrepreneurs show tenacity and willingness to fight, rather than admit defeat. However, men in agriculture and industry are more tenacious than their colleagues in finance and services. They are not only ready to wait longer but also willing to accept zero profits, or even outright losses, before considering withdrawal. The difference in attitude is the product of two factors. The first is the fixity of investment which characterizes the commodity-producing sectors. The second is the temperament of the type of man who in the first place would go knowingly into a line of activity requiring a heavy investment and who, by virtue of that choice, indicates a readiness to "stick it out" with his investment in case of adverse conditions.

The factors which the respondents most frequently said they would consider in deciding whether to withdraw were the degree of hopelessness of the situation and the presence of better alternatives into which to divert resources once the declining business was liquidated. Next in recurrence was the difficulty and expensiveness of forced liquidation. Another consideration frequently expressed was the hardship which liquidation would cause to employees, and the great hesitation the business leader would feel before inflicting such hardship. And lastly, prestige was cited as a factor delaying withdrawal even when economic wisdom dictated it. Here is a sample of the more interesting answers from individual questionnaires:

Withdrawal will only be considered if I lose my sense of achievement.

So long as I cover operating (i.e., variable) costs I will go on.

I will consider withdrawal only if I begin digging into my capital.

I will not withdraw so long as my returns, although declining, still meet my payroll and what I need to keep my family at the present level of living.

I will not withdraw, no matter how steep my losses, except if I fear that political instability is going to spoil the business climate for me.

A declining profit position is the result of bad management on the whole. If I find myself in that position, I will examine my methods carefully and try to improve them.

Only encroaching bankruptcy will make me consider pulling out.

Only nationalization of my business by government will force me out.

Losses are not possible in my line of business, except if there is mismanagement, which I will avoid.

I calculate profits on a cost-plus basis. If I am forced to lower my mark-up, I will do that and stay on so long as I make some profit. Only if I feel unable, after trying, to adjust myself to the new return will I pull out.

If profit declines, I will reorganize, rearrange inputs, change emphasis in my products and my markets. This will largely insure me against long-standing losses.

Only if financial losses are combined with my loss of interest in the business will I consider pulling out.

Closing down involves heavy termination and compensation payments. I will bear losses for a while in the hope of improvement of business rather than pull out in panic and have to make these obligatory payments to employees.

My decision will depend on my evaluation of three things: the level of general activity in the country; the degree of competition in the industry of which I am part; and the availability of promising alternatives for my resources.

My business is traditional in the family. I will not withdraw except if losses prove absolutely unbearable.

Several of these answers were combined by the respondents. But whether alone or in combination, they reveal that the yardstick of monetary profit should not be used alone in the determination of the concept of normal profit. Normal profit must incorporate other factors that together shape the decisions of businessmen.

Investment, Turnover, and Time Preference

There are many ways in which the length of the businessman's time horizon can be ascertained. The method selected in this study was to determine the preferences of the respondents with regard to the size of investment and the period of waiting for return, and with regard to the size of profit margin per unit related to a given capital turnover. The vote was divided in the proportions of 53 and 47 per cent between (a) undertakings involving heavy investment and considerable waiting before returns begin to flow in, but promising a long period of flow, and (b) undertakings involving relatively little investment, a short period of waiting, and a quick capital turnover. The nearly even division is surprising in view of the great preponderance of large-investment establishments in our universe of 207 establishments. Establishments in agriculture and industry alone number 144, and many of the establishments in services (like those of transport and hotels) require heavy investment. Together, all these establishments represent some 80 per cent of the total.

But the next question brought forth a more clear-cut expression of opinion. Strong support was given to the alternative of a small profit margin per unit of sales on a large volume of business, against the alternative of a large profit margin per unit on a small volume of business. Here it is evident that the respondents had little uncertainty as to where their preferences lay. This preference is a sign of farsightedness, inasmuch as a sales policy like the one predominantly supported builds up a valuable loyalty among clientele.

The avant-garde of the business community, the business leaders, suffer from ambivalence on the issue of investment and turnover. Many of them still have the thought patterns, habits, and inclinations that are characteristic of trade and other service sectors that are not investment-heavy. Furthermore, true to type, they are oversensitive to uncertainty, slow in accepting research as a means of extending their time horizon, and therefore excessively dependent on liquidity. Lost between the attitudes of mercantile enterprise that are proving less and less appropriate for a developing country, and those of industrial enterprise that is gradually forcing its inevitable logic on the economy, the entrepreneurial resources of Lebanon, on this issue, suffer from the strains of transition and a split personality.

THE MOTIVES OF ENTERPRISE*

The so-called "profit motive" occupies a central place in the models of economic theory and in the realm of business. Theorist and practitioner alike admit that the term "profit," or "pecuniary profit," is a shorthand symbol for a whole complex of motives, of which profit is the only one that can readily be quantified in terms of dollars and cents.[10] Serious consideration of the motives of enterprise would therefore require, at the least, the undoing of the complex and the evaluation of the relative power of each of its components. No sooner is this done than it appears that the com-

* The findings in this section are based on Tables 113, 117, 126, 133, 215–217, 225, 234–236, 244–246, 272–276, 316–318, 323, 407–409, 416, 462–464, 469. See Appendix C for list of Tables 1 through 472 and explanation of where they may be found.

ponents are not at the same logical level; some of them are further behind in the causation sequence than others. Thus, satisfaction in a sense of achievement is not at par with pecuniary profit, since the urge for achievement may manifest itself in a number of ways, of which profit-making and carving a powerful or prestigious position are only two. Be this as it may, this section reports on the inquiry into the system of evaluation espoused by the business leaders, according to which motives like those just cited, though at disparate levels if classified in a hierarchy of causation, are appraised and ranked in their influence and effectiveness.[11]

Inner Driving Forces

The respondents were requested to select, and rank, the three motives for their actions that were the most powerful, in their opinion, out of a list comprising pecuniary profit, power, prestige and status, sense of achievement, satisfaction in expansion in one's business, and philanthrophy and social service through one's money.[12] They gave the largest total vote to pecuniary profit (26.5 per cent), the next largest to the sense of achievement (23.6 per cent), and the third largest to satisfaction in expansion (17.8 per cent). The ranking of motives by respondents gave the first, second, and third places to the three motives just cited, respectively.

It is revealing of the openness of the business leaders that they flatly asserted the influence of profit considerations on their actions —just as they did in telling why they had moved into their present careers (as already reported). Without exception, whether the choices are related to age, schooling, or any other independent variable, the largest proportion of any category in any distribution has voted for pecuniary profit as the first choice. However, under this unanimity there exist different degrees of emphasis worth recording.

1) The distribution of choices by age shows that the votes for profit and achievement move in roughly opposite directions and that satisfaction in expansion in one's career, while producing a pattern roughly in line with that of achievement, is in declining

(negative) relation to age for all groups except the oldest. Generally speaking, in those cases where profit exercises a relatively weak pull, the sense of achievement, the satisfaction in expansion in one's career, and — among older men — the urge to utilize wealth for social service exercise a strong pull. The reverse is true when the pull of profit is strong. At the second and third levels of choice, power and prestige together play an important part for all age groups, but especially for men in the middle range.

2) Sector by sector, the profit motive was given proportionately the largest vote as first choice by men in agriculture, and the smallest by men in industry. It is worth noting that both in industry and in services, the vote for achievement was unusually high while that for profit was rather small.

3) In the cross-tabulation of the choices with religious affiliation, the most striking result was the markedly higher proportion of Moslems than of Christians voting for profit as first choice. A similar finding was encountered earlier in the investigation of the factors influencing the choice of career. Taking the votes for all the other motives into account, we see a larger vote among the Moslem than the Christian group for power and prestige and a larger vote among the Christians for the sense of achievement, satisfaction in expansion, and philanthropy. This distribution of votes, indicating a higher valuation of externally expressed success than of an internal sense of satisfaction, probably reflects social insecurity among the Moslems and indicates their desire to compensate for this insecurity.

4) An examination of the choices relative to the marital status of respondents and whether or not they have children reveals a greater concern for profit among married than among single men, and greater concern among married men with children than without. Married men without children put more weight than did other respondents on power, prestige, and satisfaction in expansion in one's career. (Not once did they consider philanthrophy as a first motive.) Here perhaps lies an interesting insight into the psychology

of childless men in a culture where having children is highly prestigious and emotionally rewarding. They may find compensation in certain manifestations of business success.

5) As the level of education rises, concentration on achievement also rises, but the profit motive declines in importance. Once again those motives that make for an inner sense of fulfillment exert their influence in an opposite direction to motives that strengthen the external position and status of the businessman.

6) In the distribution by form of ownership, the strength of the profit motive again contrasts with that of the achievement motive, profit being strongest in partnerships and weakest in single ownerships, and achievement being strongest in single ownerships and weakest in partnerships.

The Example of Others

The entrepreneur's evaluation of the forces that motivate him and influence the intensity and direction of his economic drive can in part be ascertained — as we have just done — from the way he describes these forces on looking inward. In part, they can also be ascertained from his evaluation of the manifestations of success, or the failings, of other entrepreneurs. When indulging in the judgment of other people, he would in effect provide a clue to the motives he holds high. Accordingly, the respondents were drawn into such judgment.

Manifestations of success. Ten manifestations of entrepreneurial success were suggested out of which the business leaders were to pick no more than four.* The four leading manifestations drew 64 per cent of the vote. Ranked according to the size of vote, they are: (1) Assurance of continuity of the business (143 votes); (2) Expansion of the business (116); (3) Introduction of important technical improvements (114); (4) Large profits (88). The concentration of opinion on these four is significant. It reveals the emphasis business leaders place on rationality, on continuity as against lucrativeness

* The ten items are given in section VIII/1 of the questionnaire (Appendix B). The vote for each is found in Table 126, which is listed in Appendix C.

in brief ventures, on growth and innovation, and — realistically — on profits.

Of the four leading signs of success, large profits are closest to the personal-focused area of motivation. Pecuniary profit can be said to be the bridge between the personal-focused and establishment-focused areas. There can be little doubt that the business leader, intent on assuring continuity for his establishment, has an interest in profit for his person as well as for the establishment which he wants to perpetuate. Although the same applies to all the manifestations, important differences exist among them on grounds of emphasis and of rationality in pursuit.

The choices made by the respondents, cross-tabulated with age, sector, religious affiliation, schooling, and form of ownership, reveal certain patterns that will be reported very briefly.

1) The very old and the very young, but more so the old, showed more appreciation of continuity than men in other age groups. On the other hand, the very young and the very old stood poles apart in their opinion of expansion, with the young most appreciative and the old least appreciative.

2) The sectors were very similar in their positions with respect to continuity, but they diverged with respect to the other leading manifestations. The commodity-producing sectors, for instance, gave technical improvement a much larger vote ratio than the services-producing sectors. The industrialists allowed this point more than twice the vote ratio allowed by the financiers; thus the two groups once again show their different interpretations of technical improvement. Wide divergence is also observed in the appraisal of profits. Among the four sectors the industrialists included the smallest proportion of respondents that considered large profits a sign of success, and had the largest proportions voting for technical improvement, improvement in product quality, and diversification of products. If it is recalled that about 63 per cent of the entrepreneurial group is in industry, it can be seen that industrial leaders, on this score, show qualities that contain good promise for innovating enterprise and for development generally.

3) There is no coherent pattern that portrays signs-of-success opinions distributed by religious affiliation.

4) Broadly speaking, as the level of schooling rises, less emphasis is put on continuity and technical improvement. Conversely, a little more is put on expansion and large profits.

5) Among the three forms of ownership, men in corporations led in emphasizing continuity and expansion. On the other hand, technical improvement drew most of its support from partnerships (the leading form in industry) and least from corporations (the leading form in finance).

The failings of others. In the belief that people reveal as considerable a part of their character by what they condemn as by what they admire, the business leaders were next asked to indicate what they considered the most notorious failings in others which they try to avoid. Thirteen such failings were suggested, and the respondent was requested to choose up to four of these.* The four which led obtained 56 per cent of the vote. They are: (1) Ostentation in personal spending (130 votes); (2) Participation in politics (107); (3) Career inconsistency, i.e., jumping from one career to another (102); (4) Lack of planning (90).

Although the failings suggested are less narrowly focused on the establishment than were the manifestations of success, and have a marked sociological bias in their content, the choices made among them are worth noting. The results obtained from this question supplement those obtained from the question on manifestations of success.

It is clear from the returns that only small numbers of the respondents concerned themselves with the business policy of other people with regard to expansion, contraction, stagnation, diffusion, or concentration. The respondents did take a position on these issues but not a strong enough position to warrant important inferences. The choice of the four leading failings is interesting mainly because of the pattern of concentration of votes it reveals.

* The thirteen failings are given in section VIII/8 of the questionnaire (Appendix B). The vote for each failing is found in Table 133, which is listed in Appendix C.

Thus, the votes for noncontinuity in career, lack of planning, or for ostentation, could hardly be controversial, whereas such matters as rapid expansion or branching off of establishments are susceptible to long, inconclusive debate concerning their "eligibility" as failings.

Several strong impressions can be reported in conclusion of this discussion of motives of enterprise. The first of these impressions is the presence of motives that are predominantly entrepreneur-directed and expressed. Some of these motives, like the satisfaction of a sense of achievement, are internally felt and weighed; some others, like profit-making, are both externally discerned and internally enjoyed. Conversely, there is a group of motives that is predominantly establishment-directed and expressed, such as assurance of continuity in the life of the establishment and success in building and controlling a smoothly operating concern. However, the differentiation between the two groups should not be carried very far, since all these motives derive from the mainspring of the entrepreneur's character and inner urges, and all of them are reflected, even if partly, in the behavior of the entrepreneur expressing itself through the establishment.

A third category of motives might be added — ones that are society-oriented or community-oriented, such as development; social service made possible through entrepreneurial success; helping entrepreneurial talent emerge; and the establishment of good relations with one's milieu. Again, these motives will not be satisfied without success in achieving the narrow targets of the establishment; and they will not be pursued unless they satisfy some personal-oriented motive. The motives of the entrepreneur and the objectives of the establishment interlock firmly.

Lastly, it is worth emphasizing that evidence has emerged from the inquiry that the profit motive stands in the minds of business leaders in clear confrontation with the achievement or inner satisfaction motive. This is particularly true at the level of first choice among the motives.

THE BUSINESS LEADER AND HIS ENVIRONMENT *

The business leader embodies in his character elements of conformity with environmental roles and sanctions, as well as elements of rebellion against them. In the absence of the conformity he would be a rebel without a base, out of context, unable to come to grips with the economic and politico-social realities of his situation. Ultimately he would flounder and fail. In the absence of rebelliousness he would not innovate. He would at best imitate but would not be instrumental in bringing about a significant rise in the rate and quality of growth in his economy.

There are many and complex relationships between the business leader and his environment — in Lebanon or anywhere else — and it would be overambitious to attempt a wide-ranging exploration of all of them.[13] Accordingly, a few selected relationships will be discussed in this section.

Economic Organization[14]

The first questions concerning the organization of the economy have to do with what structure of business appeals most to business leaders. Is it a structure characterized by *free competition* among numerous small establishments, none of which is large enough to influence the market by itself? Is it one of *limited competition* where the establishments in each industry are small in number and wield considerable power individually? Or is it one of *joint enterprise* where the state plays a major part in business through direct ownership or control of establishments?

Almost 64 per cent of the respondents preferred the free-competition type of structure, the one closest to the textbook model. Just under one third favored the model of imperfect (limited) competition, while only six men (3 per cent) favored joint enterprise. This position was encountered in reply to another question when

* The findings in this section are based on Tables 49–51, 88–92, 96–105, 107–111, 197, 201–206, 210–213, 252, 266–268, 308–312, 314, 360, 387, 394, 395, 398–404, 406, 460. See Appendix C for list of Tables 1 through 472 and explanation of where they may be found.

the business leaders indicated a preponderant opposition to ownership of public utilities by government.

Without exception, the more advanced the age group, the larger the proportion in favor of free competition. Among the sectors, it was agriculture that indicated the highest degree of preference for free competition; industry indicated the lowest preference. Finance, in this respect, stood in about the same posture as agriculture, which leads one to surmise that bankers must have understood free competition to mean not so much the existence of a large number of banks as the absence of restrictions on banking operations. Conversely, the manufacturers, wanting greater governmental protection and attention, preferred a system that provided some restrictions on the number of operators and on the degree of competition. Such a system as the manufacturers seem to envisage produces the familiar carrot-and-stick combination, except that those who expect the carrot usually believe that someone else should get the stick.

Attitudes to economic structure indicated a rising appreciation of free competition with the rise in education, except that men with graduate and professional training showed a very marked preference for limited competition. The sharp deviation of this highly educated group from positions taken by men with only undergraduate training is a phenomenon that was frequently observed in the study.

The second group of questions about economic organization sought to find out whether the respondents thought a greater degree of central planning and control of economic affairs by government would help or harm businessmen in Lebanon, and whether it would promote or retard development generally. The respondents were made to understand that planning and control did not involve state ownership of any considerable proportion of the means of production, but merely the indirect influencing of the allocation of resources.

One and a half times as many respondents were against a larger public role as were in favor. There is a striking difference between the number of respondents who favored more planning and control (81) and those who had earlier strongly opposed a mainly government-operated structure of economic organization (6). There is probably no inconsistency in these results. Planning and control must have been understood to mean little encroachment on the process of entrepreneurial decision-making, whereas outright direction must have been interpreted as the actual taking over of this process by government. The distinction is crucial for the locus of entrepreneurial authority.

The distribution of replies by age, sector, religion, and education yields several revealing results.

1) In every age group except that of 40–49, the proportion of men who believed that central planning and control would harm businessmen was larger than that of men who believed the contrary. Men in the 40–49 group were equally divided between the two opinions.

2) In each of the sectors there was proportionately more disapproval than approval of planning and control, but the commodity-producing sectors were only mildly disapproving compared with the services-producing sectors. This general picture is not surprising. In the minds of most businessmen in underdeveloped countries there is a vivid image of triumphant industrialization and intensive agriculture made possible through government efforts. But this is an image that the banker and the merchant abhor.

3) Over 55 per cent of Moslem respondents, but only 35 per cent of Christians, believed that central planning and control would help businessmen and promote development. The difference is no mere accident. It is partly a reflection of the pattern of distribution of both groups by sector, and partly of the feeling of Moslem businessmen that the present allocation of wealth and economic power is largely in favor of Christian businessmen. Central planning must have seemed to the Moslem respondents to carry the promise of a reallocation more favorable to them.

4) There was a rising disapproval of central planning with the rise in education, up to the end of undergraduate training, but the trend is reversed among those with graduate and professional train-

ing, whose attitude concerning this question is consistent with their marked preference for limited competition.

Social Approval and Politics

The respondent was asked for the attitude of his close social group toward his choice of career. Some 48 per cent of the respondents said they had met with encouragement, 28 per cent with indifference, and only 19 per cent with objection. The encouragement proportion dropped, and the objection and indifference proportions rose, with minor exceptions all the way from the age of 20 to that of 69 years. In other words, the close social group of the younger business leaders seem today to take an interest in the choice of career by their relatives or close friends greater than that taken by the social group of their older counterparts. This interest manifests itself more in encouragement than in objection. The over-all picture is one of easy sailing for the postwar crop of business leaders, especially for those heading for finance and industry. Furthermore, a larger proportion of Moslems than of Christians have received encouragement in their chosen career.

The 40 men who declared that they had met with objection thought the main grounds for objection had been the fear of uncertainty in that career, ignorance of the nature of the career, and failure to be socially impressed by the career. However, two thirds of these 40 men thought that they would meet with no similar objection if they were to start today. Among other things, this assumed change of views can mean a weakening in the grounds for objection owing to a change in the value system of society, a growing willingness to be encouraging on principle, or merely greater optimism on the part of the business leader himself. It cannot be the result of growing indifference — this would run counter to the findings.

In order to assess the importance of nonbusiness considerations in selecting personnel, we asked the respondents to state their preference among Lebanese, non-Lebanese Arab, and non-Arab technicians, given equality of training and readiness to work for the same salary. The grounds for preference were also sought. The vast majority of business leaders (82 per cent) said they would choose a Lebanese technician; 13 per cent favored a non-Arab; and only 3 men (1.4 per cent) favored a non-Lebanese Arab. These choices seem to have no significant association with age, religion, or level of education. Most respondents, when asked for their reasons, reacted quite simply by saying something like this: "But of course I would choose the Lebanese technician; he is my countryman." However, this strong emphasis on patriotism has no overtones of chauvinism. Tolerance of foreigners was amply revealed in connection with the business leaders' attitude to the entry of foreign entrepreneurs into Lebanon. Ranking next to patriotism was the expectation of better understanding vis-à-vis a compatriot owing to similarity of language and culture. Next came the conviction that the acquaintance of the Lebanese technician with local conditions would be a decisive factor in his favor. Alternatively, those declaring their preference for a non-Arab believed in the greater conscientiousness of non-Arab technicians and greater loyalty to their employer. Some respondents thought the non-Arab would display, and impose, better discipline in the fulfillment of his function.

Next, the respondents were asked if they thought it advisable for businessmen to devote some of their time and efforts to politics, "given Lebanese conditions" where — it was implied — almost everybody dabbles in politics. The respondents were strongly opposed to participation (70 per cent). A few of those favoring participation were of the opinion that it should be open, preferably through election to parliament, but most preferred indirect and covert participation, mainly through lobbying and "influence." They made no secret of their opinion of the medium through which influence can be exercised on civil servants and politicians.

A larger proportion of Moslem than of Christian respondents approved of participation in politics. Furthermore, the proportion of Moslems in favor of participation rose as the level of education rose. No coherent pattern emerges from the association of the replies with the age of the respondents.

The Business Leader and Circumstances of Operation

It remains now to evaluate the types of uncertainty that most beset enterprise, the burden of certain cost factors, the adequacy of credit facilities, and the adequacy of managerial and technical resources and of training opportunities.

The respondents were asked to choose among five types of uncertainty the ones that influenced them most in their entrepreneurial decisions, and then to rank their choices. The types suggested were:

1) Uncertainty deriving from political conditions (discontinuity of policy, arbitrary change of policy, nepotism, and so on).

2) Uncertainty deriving from changes in tastes and markets and the inability to tell the future of demand.

3) Uncertainty deriving from frequent changes in tariffs and taxes.

4) Uncertainty deriving from technical change.

5) Uncertainty deriving from changes in costs of inputs.

In all, 276 choices were made, of which 207 (i.e., by all respondents) were for first place, 55 for second place, 11 for third place, and 3 for fourth place. Out of the total of 276, political uncertainty got 171. And out of the 207 votes for first place, the same type got 163. The weight of political uncertainty in the scales of business hardly needs any justification or proof. In Lebanon the political factor has more than usual weight for the business leader because of his heavy dependence on the state of stability beyond Lebanon in the Middle East, and on the extent of cooperation among Middle Eastern countries.

When the respondents were asked what they considered a satisfactory protection against uncertainty, some of them declared that no protection was possible against the uncertainty that caused them anxiety; others felt that a list of reactions suggested in the questionnaire did not apply to them; still others refused to answer the question. But the more optimistic (who were in a majority) put their faith in diversification as a protective measure — diversification in products, in location of business interests, and in sectors. Next to that they emphasized liquidity.

The very young business leaders were heavily in favor of diversification but gave little weight to liquidity; the very old stood on the other side of the fence on both scores. Among the sectors, manufacturers shunned liquidity as a protection while financiers favored it. The agriculturists, unexpectedly, also favored liquidity. On the question of input costs and their impact on operations, little need be said here, because the findings were rather uniform with regard to all the items examined. The respondent was asked whether certain factors were favorable, unfavorable, or "indifferent" to the expansion of his business. The list of factors given to him was: the salary and wage level, interest rates, the tax system, the tax level, tariff rates, and labor legislation. All except one were declared either outright favorable for expansion or of indifferent effect. Only labor legislation was thought by a majority as an unfavorable factor. On the whole, the entrepreneurial group display a forceful attitude and a confident outlook. In the face of growing difficulty to export, they do not express themselves in accusatory terms nor lay blame on this or that input cost. More than merely accepting these costs, they believe them satisfactory or neutral and turn to their fight for markets.

The prevailing shortage of credit facilities for medium-term and long-term loans was felt by over two thirds of the respondents. Agriculturists and manufacturers felt the shortage more keenly than men in services and finance. As for the shortage of skilled personnel, the business leader was given a list of five possible ways of raising the level of technical knowledge, and was asked to check one or more, applicable to his field. About three fifths of the vote concentrated on two suggestions: sending students and other trainees abroad for training, and bringing foreign scientists and technicians to train nationals on the job. On the other hand, the smallest number of votes went to the suggestion that technical training be undertaken in government institutions; interestingly enough, none of those votes came from men in the 20–29 and 60–69 age groups. But though in agreement on what policies to refuse, these two groups chose different suggestions as their favored policy: the young mainly choosing training on the job, the old choosing training in institutions established by the business community. Differentiated by the educational level of the respondents, the replies fail to produce any clear pattern.

The respondent was also asked if, in his field of business, there were enough able managers, able foremen or supervisors, and technicians and skilled workers. In each case the business leaders were asked for their views regarding the best way of training these cadres and whether or not training facilities existed in the establishments. Without exception, the number of respondents who declared a shortage of skilled personnel at every level of skill far exceeded the number expressing satisfaction with the supply. The shortages notwithstanding, only one third of the respondents stated that they provided some formal training at their expense for their personnel, apart from training acquired in the performance of the job. Most such training — for what it is worth — is in corporations, and in service enterprises and banks. Neither the education nor the age structure of respondents showed a clear-cut association with the provision of training facilities.

All in all, what the business leaders said about their environment fits into the general picture of the social and political setting of enterprise in Lebanon, given in our first chapter. From a combination of the detailed data and the general survey come the following observations.

The entrepreneurial group in Lebanon is characterized by a high degree of exposure to outside factors. The exposure has resulted from long association with foreigners, intensified through education and travel. There is no resentment against the obvious manifestations of Westernization in Lebanon; on the contrary, there is even pride in them.

The limitation of the local market and the scarcity of natural resources, pressing on an energetic business group, make for an expansive outlook and temperament. This expansiveness expresses itself in the urge for the growth of establishments as well as in diversification, improvement of quality, and geographical mobility. And all the while, the pressure to expand provokes a brisk competitiveness and a desire to keep the channels to competition open and unobstructed.

In this limited sense, Lebanese business leaders feel at home in their traditional economic and social molds, and conformity rather than rebellion is the result. Where they have rebelled is in shifting away from the traditional activities of trade, small finance, and personal services toward industry, banking, intensive agriculture, transport, and professional services like insurance and advertising. Rebellion also appears in the field of human relations, where the businessman moves away, even if slowly, from the pressure of personal considerations and kinship toward a system of choice of staff by merit according to impersonal rules and standards.

In all this the impact of the environment on the business leader is obviously great. Yet it is only one side of the interaction between the two. The other side — the impact of the business leader on his environment — takes us back to the fundamental question of the initiation of the process of development.

Chapter 5

ENTERPRISE FOR DEVELOPMENT

THE PRESENT inquiry took its departure from a broad conceptual framework. Data related to this framework were collected through interviews with business leaders in the whole of Lebanon, and inferences have since been drawn from the data. Measured against the expectations expressed, or implied, in the framework, the inferences reported in Chapter 4 must seem quite limited in scope.

However, I feel that no regrets need be expressed on this account. Field research concerning the entrepreneurial resources of a whole country and their part in development is extremely rare. The attempt to draw a framework suitable for such research can be useful in itself, even if the conclusions that emerge are of limited reach. The conduct of more studies for more countries would permit generalization both on entrepreneurship and on development that a one-country study permits only tentatively and within limitations. To borrow from economic theory, "external economies" can be expected to arise from the formulation of a conceptual framework that looks too big and wasteful for the purposes of one inquiry only, if this framework is used for further inquiries in more countries.

The findings of the present study in themselves warn us against venturing to suggest the entrepreneur as the master key to a theory of development, in the broad sense in which development has been defined in this book — namely as a large and sustained increase in the rate of growth of slowly growing economies that cannot be achieved unless important changes occur in technology and in social and political institutions. In this sense, neither the approach nor the conclusions are Schumpeterian. But to say this is not to deny the significance of the role of entrepreneurship in the process of development; it is, instead, to indicate the necessity of exploring the nature and the timing of the role in the unfolding of this process.

Certain broad conclusions can be drawn from the empirical findings of the inquiry, and some speculation can be made which is not directly based on the data but which flows from the original concepts and views underlying the inquiry, as qualified or confirmed by the general trend of the findings. The conclusions and the speculation fall into two groups. The first, more concluding than speculating, relates largely to the operation of enterprise and entrepreneurs in Lebanon. The second, more speculating than concluding, relates to the place of enterprise in the whole process of development. In this latter connection generalizations will be made from the one case of Lebanon, tentatively of course but perhaps not without justification.

In the area of entrepreneurial theory this study has relaxed the Schumpeterian definition of entrepreneurship and broadened its horizon. The result has both theoretical interest and practical implications for underdeveloped countries.

The findings suggest the acceptance of the idea that the content of entrepreneurial decisions may just be the adaptation and derivation of innovations made elsewhere. Accordingly, the dramatic and rare figure of the entrepreneur in the Schumpeterian tradition becomes the more common adapter, the business leader acting alone or in a team, whether as capital-owner, top executive, or a mere department head. Furthermore, enterprise involves not only spectacular innovations calling forth lumpy investments of massive implication, introduced sporadically, but also modest innovations on an ever widening front in production technology, marketing, organization, public relations, internal communication, and the system of decision-making itself — small innovations with no massive implications if viewed individually but with a strong, economy-wide impact in the aggregate.

This shift in outlook is not the outcome of a contention that the underdeveloped world calls for a body of theory altogether different from the one relevant to the developed world. It is rather a reflection of the conviction, confirmed by the present study, that the marked differences between these two worlds call for qualifications in the theory of enterprise as elaborated and known in the Western world. Thus we neither have, nor need, two theories of enterprise, but one theory that is "open at both ends" — to borrow a phrase from Arthur H. Cole. An open-end view of enterprise can be used for the analysis of conditions in different societies at any one time but at different levels of development, and at different points in history whether or not at different levels of development. In this sense, the study claims to add to the length of the open-end view in order that it may become more usable for a phase of development not well served by existing theory.

Any definition of entrepreneurship assumes a particular locus of enterprise consistent with it. If, therefore, the entrepreneurial function is to be found in the widespread areas of adaptation and derivation in technology, organization, marketing, and public relations, it follows that enterprise may indeed reside at the level of decision in *any* of these several areas and the function may well be discharged by men below the man who is at the very top of the pyramid of authority.

The practical implication of these definitional variations must be obvious by now. It is frequently said that the training of managers is feasible but that the training of entrepreneurs is almost impossible. This is a reflection of the notion that managerial ability is something that can be taught to the young executive, in business schools and through experience, but that a man is born an entrepreneur. I submit that in the modern world the distinction is not so clear-cut; and, considering the changed function of the entrepreneur, as indicated in this study, and the extended locus of enterprise, the manpower base from which entrepreneurial resources can be drawn can indeed be conditioned to produce entrepreneurial talent. Furthermore, the volume of the flow of entrepreneurial ideas can more easily be influenced owing to the ramification of the tributaries to this flow: in other words, we no more have just one stream coming from the business leader in person but several smaller streams converging and meeting in the establishment and in the industry.

In practice, a developing society can act on two fronts for the purpose of increasing this flow of ideas. It can remove impediments in the way of the flow by providing such facilities as are likely to expose businessmen to new ideas—expose not only established businessmen but also young men in the process of choosing a career. Second, it can contribute directly to the flow of entrepreneurial ideas through specially established agencies. The function of these agencies, which in varying forms have appeared in the Middle East and in Latin America, is to look for industries that have a fair chance of viability. Cost-and-market studies and viability appraisals are then made for such industries. If the results are favorable, the studies are made available to anybody interested in them. The initial ideas do not necessarily originate in the agency but frequently originate in the business community. In the latter case they receive equal attention and study if they have prima facie value. Such activity in the public sector has proved valuable in speeding up the emergence of entrepreneurs and in adding to the flow of entrepreneurial ideas capable of being used in business.

The relaxation of definitions that we are discussing is also relevant to the strong drive for development characterizing most underdeveloped countries of our day. Regardless of the degree of success of such drives, invariably they add to the social overhead capital and extend the rule of law and order in a country to a measure that usually reduces the environmental impediments to the emergence of enterprise. (Where in its eagerness to step up the rate of growth a government encroaches on the field of activity conventionally claimed by private enterprise, thus inhibiting entrepreneurs, it creates a situation no worse than that preceding its development program.) In circumstances made more favorable for business through governmental development efforts, the flow of enterprise is likely to be increased and speeded up. Once the emergence of private entrepreneurs begins to a noticeable extent, the process can normally be expected to become cumulative.

The point can be illustrated in several other ways. But the areas of action referred to should suffice to show the manner in which a relaxation of the definition of enterprise and of its locus can improve our understanding of what goes on in the underdeveloped world and can guide the policy-maker in his effort to promote the stepping up of entrepreneurial activity in the country. The argument may be stated simply in the following way. If men introducing epoch-making innovations are the only ones who can be considered entrepreneurs, and if entrepreneurship is a strategic factor in development, then underdeveloped countries are all doomed to a slow rate of growth if not to stagnation. The fact that in the real world around us many of these countries appear far from doomed necessitates a reappraisal both of the theory of entrepreneurship and of development. The reappraisal has been attempted in this book.

If I were asked to emphasize one point upon which I have emerged from the study more convinced than before I would single out the importance of rational and efficient organization in the establishment as a necessary adjunct to innovation, no matter how variously defined or where in the establishment such innovation is located. Organization without innovation remains dead, a battery without a spark. Innovation without an appropriate organization around it is an uncaptured, a lost, spark. The entrepreneurs of a country may well be judged according to the extent to which they have realized the relationship between innovation and organization.

This realization is evident in Lebanon; the majority of the business leaders interviewed understood the nature and implications of the relationship. No aspect of their function did they emphasize as strongly and consistently as conception of new ideas within an advanced organizational design that embodies the ideas and furthers their success.

The implications of this emphasis reach far into the structure, the locus, the quality, and the motives of enterprise, as well as into the ability of entrepreneurial resources to meet crises and to respond to challenges emanating from the environment or from enterprise itself in its dynamic restlessness. Regardless of the sector in which entrepreneurial activity is manifested, the adoption of forms of organization and of authority-sharing formulas best suited to the activity undertaken and to its targets and problems is a touchstone of successful enterprise. The form may be that of single ownership, partnership, or corporation. The formula may be one of monolithic concentration, of sharing of authority among equals, or of institutionalization in a hierarchy where decisions are dispersed yet integrated according to a master plan. What determines the form and the formula is the stage of development of enterprise and in turn society's general level of organization and development. On both scores, it can be said that Lebanon is crossing over into a stage of institutional organization.

By its very nature this crossing over requires a coexistence of the backward with the advancing and the advanced. The features of transition are plentiful, as was illustrated in the preceding chapter, particularly in the section dealing with the quality of enterprise in Lebanon. However, what sets the tone of business leadership is that segment of enterprise which is ahead of the rest in the refinement and performance of its organization. Owing to the large size and the efficiency of this segment, my estimate is that the transition of the bulk of entrepreneurial resources to institutional organization is easily within reach in Lebanon.

There is good evidence that this transition is now being made. Since the Second World War there has been an upsurge in entrepreneurial activity which has attracted young, well-educated, widely traveled men. These men have moved mainly into new manufacturing and specialized services industries, and into full-fledged banking. Many, especially among manufacturers, have come into their entrepreneurial careers right after school or college — in fact the tendency seems to be growing in recent years for young men to go into independent business without prior apprenticeship in other people's establishments. Those who have come from a nonentrepreneurial business career have had experience mainly in trade, elementary industry, the professions, and services; few have been landlords or are the sons of landlords. No serious taboos or social prejudices have blocked this movement, and mobility between social groups and between economic activities and sectors is markedly easy.

That there still are islands of resistance to new types of economic activity and organization cannot be denied. Witness the parallel, persistent appeal to businessmen of trade and traditional services, an appeal which is reflected in the active relations business leaders keep with these older activities despite their entry into the newer nontraditional activities. Admittedly, continued association with the mercantile roots of enterprise is valuable, since trade remains an important reservoir of entrepreneurial talent. Yet the association carries with it a duality of attitude and creates contradictions in the quality of enterprise.

These contradictions are manifest in certain positions taken by a number of entrepreneurs in the industrial sector, which are obviously left-overs from a trading background. An illustration of these positions is the distaste for heavy investment and impatience with the slow flow of returns from such investment. The contradictions are also manifest in the disregard by certain leaders, irrespective of sector, of those professional services and practices on which the entrepreneur can draw in making his decisions. A third manifestation — partly explainable by the scarcity of entrepreneurial resources — is encountered in the diffusion of the activities of entrepreneurs. The "general entrepreneur" extends his interests and activities into several sectors or industries, as many before him have done elsewhere at similar stages of entrepreneurial development. Under these circumstances neither purity of entrepreneurial types (making for specificity in areas of action), nor universality (making for diffusion), need exist in isolation. What we have is a hybrid of both types. Under many a specialized entrepreneur one can find hidden a general entrepreneur who will take over and dominate the other self if conditions permit. Diversity of types characterizes a large part of the entrepreneurial group.

Surveyed broadly, entrepreneurial resources in Lebanon display valuable qualities of daring and a strong innovational bent. Furthermore, they now promote the organizational patterns necessary to sustain the innovations introduced and the professional services that provide the degree of rationality required for the survival and success of establishments. Hence the relative popularity of the corporation among business leaders, and of cost accounting, external audit, insurance, and technical literature in corporate establishments. Both the special merits of the corporation and the inclinations of those entrepreneurs who choose the corporate form of business emerge quite clearly in the study. As a result of these personal inclinations and the inherent advantages of corporate structure we witness an increasing degree of sharing and delegation of authority; an awareness of the role of communication between management and labor; a reasonably widespread use of professional services; a promising tendency to provide training facilities for employees; a growing measure of tolerance toward non–capital-owning management; and a definite willingness to consult experts and staff, rather than friends and relatives, on business matters.

Other important qualities characterizing enterprise in Lebanon are dogged persistence in the face of unpromising conditions (such as bad business and a drop in profits) and versatility and resourcefulness in switching over to new products or processes that promise to pull the establishment out of its difficulty. Both the doggedness and the versatility on the whole reflect a lengthening of the time horizon of business leaders, strong attachment to the establishment, and concern for its continuity. In other words, the predominant pattern of brief, highly lucrative transactions characterizing a mercantile community is giving way, even if slowly, to one of longer-term undertakings the continuity of which is a strong desideratum.

Whether as a general or a specialized entrepreneur, as a lone operator or an organization man, as a businessman-entrepreneur or a technician-entrepreneur, the business leader in Lebanon seems to be reasonably well-informed. He is far from the legendary coffee-house as a center for the collection and diffusion of business information. He buys technical literature, corresponds with his external supply and market contacts, keeps up active — even if narrowly focused — relations with his professional associates, travels abroad frequently, and visits fairs and exhibitions. He tries to keep his entrepreneurial spirit young and his business faculties sharp and creative.

While possessing a robust interest in monetary profit, the business leader in Lebanon has compelling nonpecuniary objectives. He has a strong desire to excel in terms of technical improvement and quality of product. He is motivated by an urge for achievement and finds a satisfaction in carrying the establishment along a path of success distinct from the satisfaction of making money in the process. The continuity of the establishment, as has just been stated, is of great significance to him. The motives centered around his person blend with those centered around his establishment. However, he is not yet society-centered or even community-centered. He makes few and small, if any, donations to charity drives not linked closely with his narrow community. He sets up no research or education funds, and he finances no study programs that are not part of his profit-making operations. His interest in politics is keen, though he considers businessmen's participation in politics wrong. But this interest is on the whole geared to his own business or to his industry. His national consciousness does not seem to lead him as yet to accept certain financial sacrifices for the general good.

Cultural heritage and environmental factors have strongly determined both the volume and the quality of entrepreneurial resources in Lebanon. The long-standing openness of society and its exposure to Western influences, and the resulting flexibility in attitudes and mobility of factors of production — notwithstanding internal denominational fragmentation — have produced the right atmosphere for the emergence of an entrepreneurial class in the volume and with the traits that we see today. The political independence of the country right after the Second World War, and the adoption by government of economic policies largely in agreement with businessmen's desires, have provided the business community with the right political framework for its intensified activity. Education and travel have expanded the horizons and enhanced the inventiveness of potential entrepreneurs. The confidence that effort will be well rewarded and that the reward will not be snatched away either by government or by unlawful acts of individuals, coupled with a firm belief in private enterprise in business and government circles alike, have added to the forces that promote enterprise in Lebanon.

Openness to the outside world has also brought about a marked tolerance toward foreign enterprise in the country. The non-Lebanese businessman still finds himself quite welcome in the economy, although there is a growing tendency to limit this welcome to the man with new ideas not yet embodied in local establishments. As a result of this willingness to accept and to assimilate foreign entrepreneurs, individually or as members of minority groups, the stream of enterprise has been enriched. The position and the role of these foreigners and minority groups, whether or not they have allowed themselves to be assimilated, have not been menaced or seriously upset by the varied political experiences of the past few decades, either in Lebanon or in the rest of the Middle East.

Remarkable as they are by the standards of the underdeveloped world, the business leaders of Lebanon cannot claim the credit for their country's prosperity. Many factors are involved. The interaction and interdependence of these factors make it extremely difficult, if not impossible, to assign to each of the factors its relative weight at any one moment. It is easier to trace the change over a period of time in the significance of a particular factor, since such a change can reflect a discernible transformation in the circumstances surrounding the process of development. It is the relative ease with which this transformation can be observed and analyzed that makes it possible to weigh the role of entrepreneurship at various points in the process.

In what remains of this chapter, I will attempt to evaluate the role of the entrepreneurial group in Lebanon and, at the risk of treading on less firm ground, to make some comments about the entrepreneur's role in the process of development in underdeveloped countries generally. In this whole discussion there will be a confrontation of the entrepreneurial factor with nonentrepreneurial factors, since the purpose of the analysis is to examine the validity of the contention that the entrepreneur is not only a strategic factor, but the prime mover, in development. Originally taken by Schumpeter, this position still represents the conviction of many writers on the subject of enterprise.

It is essential for the sake of analysis to keep two variables apart: the role of entrepreneurship, other things assumed given; and the same role, other things allowed to be in motion. Expressed differently, we have here two issues. The first is the role of entrepreneurship in bringing about development in an appropriate setting already prepared by society. The other is the role in the absence of such a setting; that is, the issue of whether entrepreneurship in itself can be instrumental in putting in motion the forces and factors that prepare the setting. Speculation on the nature of these issues leads me to the following concluding remarks.

Little controversy, if any, will be aroused by the statement that entrepreneurship is a strategic factor of development in a setting where everything else is propitious: the existence of law and order, acceptance of new technology, rising education, an open social system, appropriate business legislation, adequate capital goods and foreign exchanges, and a decent-sized market — to name only a few favorable circumstances. Anybody disagreeing with this statement will probably do so because it seems to imply that the entrepreneurial resources, ready for action, will sit by and wait for the emergence of circumstances favorable to enterprise. As a piece of mental exercise such a scheme of affairs depicting a propitious setting is unobjectionable. As a lesson about the real world it is barren and unhelpful.

We should move, then, to the question of the role of entrepreneurship in the whole chain of causation leading from stagnation to that deep stir in society which makes development possible. Only by doing this can we evaluate that role in a situation where the setting is not prepared for development.

Without subscribing to an extreme theory of economic determinism one can say that the role of entrepreneurship as a major economic force which greatly influences environment via change in the economy is important and obvious. Yet it is one thing for economic forces to have great influence and another for them to be the motive power, the prime mover, in shaping society and setting the pace of progress. Economic forces, spearheaded by the entrepreneurial class, are one influence among several and probably are not the prime mover at all.

Several observations can be marshaled in support of this thesis. There is, first, the low level of economic motivation in underdeveloped countries, where the *homo oeconomicus* of classical economic theory would find himself quite ill at ease. And the greater the degree of underdevelopment, the truer this statement. Not infrequently in these countries economic common sense is overwhelmed by emotional and political pressures. The fact that these pressures are often created by political operators and are not internally and spontaneously generated within the system of behavior of the masses is immaterial to the argument. Nor does the fact of the business leaders' marked economic motivation defeat the argument, since businessmen in underdeveloped countries are generally more interested in short-term, mercantile transactions than the long-term investment and organizational continuity that are required for development.

In the second place, strong as their pecuniary and other motives may be, business leaders are very much a minority in underdeveloped countries and they do not have the means to prepare a favorable setting for their own activities. Such a setting involves reforms in the political system and in the conduct of government, the absorption of new scientific and technical findings by society, the promotion of education, the change of attitudes at all levels of manpower, and improvement in the economic system at large. The more underdeveloped the country and the smaller its entrepreneurial class, the less will that class be able to provide a favorable setting. In fact, considering the shortsightedness of enterprise in backward societies and the dubiousness of circumstances which usually give rise to businessmen's profits, it is doubtful whether the business community would be eager to have a reformed and honest government and an open social system.

In the third place, even assuming the best of intentions on the part of established businessmen, we would still be left with a fundamental question: Can businessmen, as the decision-centers of economic forces, ignite the *first* spark that brings to life society's desire for significant change in a large number of aspects of its life and thus set the process of development in motion? Even if we take into account the exceptional qualities of entrepreneurs and their propensity to rebel against the traditional limitations of their environment and to strive for change, our answer will still be in the negative. The argument in support of this position is quite simple. The desires and motives of entrepreneurs are far too narrow and limited, and their power and influence too self-centered and suspect, to be a decisive factor in generating the desire in society for radical change on the several social and political fronts. And nothing less can create the framework for development and set in motion the process of transition from stagnation to growth and development.

The experience of Lebanon can be used to illustrate the point. The country is fortunate, by the standards of underdeveloped countries, in having a large and capable entrepreneurial group. The economy is developing within a broad framework of social and political institutions and attitudes favorable to economic expansion. Yet, well placed as the entrepreneurs in Lebanon are, they cannot claim credit for the social and technological breakthroughs that have occurred since the Second World War. They have benefited from long exposure to the West, from better educational facilities than in most other places in Asia and Africa, from their geography and scenery. There is little doubt that the entrepreneurial class has been quick to capitalize on all the favorable factors in its environment. But it must be remembered that these factors made their appearance long before the expansion in entrepreneurial activity and the take-off into development of the past decade and a half.

The interviewing conducted for the present study revealed how little the entrepreneurs had done for the construction and consolidation of the very framework without which their activity would have been impossible. Thus, most of the training of personnel, from the foreman upwards, has been done by nonbusiness institutions or acquired through personal effort. Powerful as it is, the entrepreneurial class admits its complete dependence on the political forces running the country and on the continuance of the rule of law and of political stability. While declaring serious dissatisfaction with the level and quality of education and with many of the country's economic laws, the entrepreneur can suggest no formula for correcting the situation, notwithstanding his heavy reliance on the education and the laws with which he is dissatisfied.

We must not look for a paradox here. The situation conforms with what we should expect it to be. Even though the entrepreneur may have more say in the matter of social and political reform than the school teacher, the foreman, the poet, or the architect, he does not have enough power to set in motion the forces that bring about the building of the framework of development in a society that is still backward.

What applies to Lebanon applies more forcefully to less developed countries. Most of these faced the postwar world from an economic and a social position of greater disadvantage than did Lebanon. The urge for development in these countries could not but have carried with it a greater element of desperation and, in the nature of the case, of frenzied eagerness for drastic action. In the circumstances, the entrepreneurial class — where it existed in an embryonic state — must have had even less power than in Lebanon to set in motion the forces of fundamental change.

This power must be sought outside and beyond entrepreneurship and economics. The present study was not designed for the purposes of such a search; nevertheless, my concern with the relation between entrepreneurship and development perhaps justifies some speculation.

I submit that the starting point, the source of forces of fundamental change, lies in the realm of ideas broadly defined — ideas that create dissatisfaction with physical need and social degradation, and that move thinkers, reformers, social-minded politicians, and activists generally to act or at least to press for action. The force of dissatisfaction may be released by a military humiliation that underlines the country's backwardness and weakness, or by the success of a country in its struggle for liberation from foreign rule, or it may express one aspect of a nationalist movement turned insurgent, or may simply be set in motion by intense envy of more prosperous nations. In any case dissatisfaction on the part of articulate groups (among which army officers play no small part in the underdeveloped countries of today) disturbs the stagnation of society's life and acts with the power of a shock on most literate citizens. Intensified awareness of the country's state of backwardness, poverty, social deprivation, or military and political weakness forces on the ruling group a sense of responsibility. This sense may be short-lived; it may lead to quixotic gestures; it may result in over-reaching and suicidal acts. Nonetheless it will generally let loose an insistent demand by the articulate and active groups in society for social action geared in one of its aspects to the improvement of economic conditions.

From here on the sequence is not difficult to imagine. Barring a decisive frustration at an early stage of the desire and demand for reform, measures will begin to be enacted in response to the challenge of backwardness, even by a predatory and reactionary oligarchy. A ruling group moderately sensitive to public sentiment and public pressures will move to act — whether from genuine concern for public welfare, in self-defense, or to catch up, nationally speaking, with the Joneses. A breakthrough somewhere in the resistance to social change will be made.

As one area of reform after another is conquered and widened, the environment becomes more and more clement to enterprise. At the beginning only the more daring and imaginative of entrepreneurs will emerge. As the environment begins to satisfy yet more favorable conditions for business, larger numbers of entrepreneurs will appear, act, and press for more reform; in the aggregate their activities will cause economic change and improvement in the performance of the economy. This success will make the plea for yet broader reform more insistent and at the same time make the operation of the reform economically more feasible through the growth in national product. And so on from one round to the next.

Admittedly, this is an oversimplified description of the process of change. Nevertheless, the experience of societies that have stepped out of their economic and social stagnation and moved over the threshold of development largely supports this thesis. This is not the place to argue the case at length, although the experience of Japan, Mexico, Turkey, India, and Egypt, as much as the failure of many other countries to enter the phase of development or to move toward it, can be cited in support of the thesis.*

* In "Development: The Visible or the Invisible Hand?" (*World Politics,* July 1961), I have examined in some detail the process of development and the respective roles of economic and noneconomic forces in initiating development.

The entrepreneur, then, appears to be the beneficiary of the initial effect of the complex of primary forces making for reform, *not* a primary force himself. Nevertheless, he is not a parasite, a passive receiver of unearned benefits. No sooner does the environment permit his emergence than he begins to act and to put back into the process of reform some of the fruits of his performance in the shape of improved and diversified economic units and techniques of production and distribution, as well as economic and technological institutions and services necessary for further advances in the economy's performance — in addition to an increased national product on which the government can draw.

Although the emergence and the performance of the entrepreneur are an outcome of a complex of other forces in action, development is inconceivable without him in a system of private enterprise. The preparation of the environmental setting will fail to lead to the economic end product unless the economic operator emerges and performs his role satisfactorily. Without him, the stage will remain without the actor, unused. To carry the metaphor a little further, the playwright, director, light engineer, and stage hands are no substitute for the actor.

If he does not come to the center of the stage the government will most probably step in. In some cases it has done so even when entrepreneurs were ready to fill the bill. But that is another problem, and neither the entrepreneur nor the economist can do much about it in underdeveloped countries. Having done a great deal to prepare the setting, the government may feel entitled, or even in duty bound, to have a predominant and active say in the manner in which the role is played.

If the entrepreneur makes his entry unobstructed, he will certainly be the beneficiary of the trouble and toil that have gone into the preparation of the setting, but he will also be a factor in the further reshaping of the setting for future generations of actors. He is a strategic factor in development; he is not the initiator of development. This is perhaps the principal lesson of the present study. And its applicability goes far beyond Lebanon.

APPENDIX A

Introductory Letter Sent to Business Leaders To Be Interviewed

AMERICAN UNIVERSITY OF BEIRUT

BEIRUT — LEBANON

Department of Economics Telephone 30822
Economic Research Institute Beirut, ...

Dear. . . .

The Economic Research Institute of the American University of Beirut is undertaking an academic study of the part that leading businessmen play in the development of Lebanon. In order to do this we are interviewing a select number of the most prominent businessmen in the country, and your name is one of those on our list.

This study, it is hoped, will greatly help in the understanding of the Lebanese economy and how it functions through the decisions of entrepreneurs in the fields of trade, industry, finance, agriculture, transport, and services. It will also help promote future development through the collection of economic data that will be made available, in aggregate form in the final report, to businessmen and to public bodies interested in the economic affairs of the country.

We would appreciate it very much if you could support the study by giving us an interview within the next few weeks. We will be contacting you shortly in order to know when it would be convenient for you to grant us this interview.

Yours very truly,

Yusif A. Sayigh
Director
Economic Research Institute

APPENDIX B

Questionnaire Used in Interviews

I. INTRODUCTORY: THE ENTREPRENEUR AND THE ESTABLISHMENT

A. *Personal Information*

1. Name of respondent
2. Position (or title) in Establishment
3. Date of birth
4. Place of birth (Specify village, city, country)
5. Marital status: Single Married Separated Divorced Widowed
6. If married, number of children
7. If respondent not sole owner of Establishment, name of owner(s) (unless Establishment is a corporation)

B. *The Establishment*

1. Registered name of Establishment
2. Date of founding of present Establishment
3. Date at which respondent took office
4. Has Establishment changed ownership? (if not corporation) Yes. No.
5. If yes, specify change

C. *Field of Activity*

1. What line(s) of business is Establishment engaged in? (Check one or more)
   - a. Agriculture
   - b. Industry
   - c. Construction and real estate
   - d. Trade
   - e. Finance
   - f. Transport
   - g. Other Services
   - h. Other (specify)
2. What product(s) (goods or services) does Establishment produce or offer?
3. List other Establishments, in Lebanon and outside, in which you have direct participation as partner or member of board of directors or outright owner, and indicate nature of participation:

Establishment *Nature of Participation*

a.
b.
c.
d.
e

4. What is the peak number of employees in the Establishment?
   Staff Labourers

D. *Form of Ownership*

1. What is the form of ownership of the Establishment?
   a. Individual proprietorship
   b. Partnership of the "nom-collectif" type
   c. Partnership of the "société en commandite — simple" type
   d. Partnership of the "société en commandite — par action" type
   e. Corporation (Société anonyme)

E. *Capital and Finance of Establishment*

At founding *Now*

1. State the nominal, registered capital:
2. Paid-up capital
3. How was capital (or finance) raised? (Check one or more)
   a. Resources of owner(s)
   b. Borrowing from relatives
   c. Borrowing from other individuals
   d. Borrowing from banks
   e. Sale of stock (or subscription stock)
   f. Sale of bonds
   g. Other (specify)
4. If part or all of capital came from owner's resources, was that from another business? Yes. No.
5. If yes, specify sector or sectors
6. If from owner's or family resources, but not from another business, indicate source or sources (Check one or more)
   a. Sale of property
   b. Gift from parents
   c. Inheritance
   d. Other (specify)

II. FORM AND LOCUS OF ENTREPRENEURSHIP

A. *Entrepreneurial Function*

1. As the person taking important decisions in the Establishment, what do you conceive your function or functions to be: (Check the four most important, in that order)
   a. Conception of the idea of the business
   b. Designing the process of operation
   c. Designing the organization (administration of various processes of production, marketing, research, etc.)
   d. Provision of capital
   e. Setting up of Establishment
   f. Choice of product(s) to produce or offer
   g. Employment of resources (human and material) and their coordination

h. Technical decisions (choice of machines, processes, etc.)
i. Decisions regarding selling policy and methods, and advertising
j. Price fixing and quantity fixing
k. Finding new markets and setting up of branches
l. Management of Establishment
m. Termination of business
n. Other (specify)

2. What is the innovation you have introduced into the Establishment, or for which you created the Establishment?

B. *Locus of Entrepreneurial Responsibility*

1. Are there employees in the Establishment who make entrepreneurial decisions? Yes. No.
2. If yes, indicate his (their) title(s) and functions:

	Title	*Function*
a.		
b.		
c.		
d.		

3. If your authority itself is jointly shared, indicate who by:
   a. Partner(s)
   b. Board of directors
   c. Creditors
4. What are the powers of the person(s) sharing authority with you?
   a. Joint decisions
   b. Veto power
   c. Power to decide when issue is of a certain magnitude
   d. Power to decide in certain areas on the basis of division of labour
   e. Other (specify)
5. Is the administration divided into sections or departments on the basis of different areas of operation? Yes. No.
6. If yes, please check which of these:
   a. Production (including technical section)
   b. Marketing (including advertising)
   c. Administration (including personnel)
   d. Finance
   e. Research
   f. Other (specify)
7. Does your Establishment have any independent branches, or branches that constitute an integral part of the operations of the Establishment? Yes. No.
8. If Establishment is either a principal or a branch, define the limits of your authority vis-à-vis the branches or the principal, as the case may be:

III. ORIGINS AND MOBILITY OF ENTREPRENEURS AND OF ENTREPRENEURIAL IDEAS

A. *Entrepreneur's Background*

1. Give a brief history of your education:

a. School	From	To
Degree obtained		
b. School	From	To
Degree obtained		

c. School From To
Degree obtained
d. School From To
Degree obtained
(N.B. School means school or university. Please indicate location of institution.)

2. What is your present nationality?
3. What was your father's original nationality?
4. If you are of non-Lebanese origin:
   a. From which country did you emigrate?
   b. When did you emigrate?
   c. Under what circumstances did you emigrate? (That is, reasons for leaving)
   d. What made you choose Lebanon?
5. What is (was) your father's business or occupation?
6. Is there a tradition in the family to run that type of business (or career)? Yes. No.
7. If yes, since when? (For how many generations?)
8. What are (were) your father's important sources of income?
   a. b.
   c. d.
9. Did you work for another entrepreneur before? Yes. No.
10. If yes, who?
11. Date at which you started business as entrepreneur (any business)
    present business

B. *Origin of the Entrepreneurial Idea*

1. Did you have any training (other than school education or on-the-job training), for any profession, occupation, craft or business? Yes. No.
2. If yes, state:
   a. Type of training
   b. Place of training
   c. Duration of training years, from to
3. Did you travel outside Lebanon or Syria (or outside your country of origin if not of Lebanese or Syrian origin) before starting your present business career? Yes. No.
4. If yes, state:

	Places travelled to	*Duration of trip (and year if possible)*	*Purpose*
a.			
b.			
c.			
d.			

(N.B. The purposes are education, recreation, business experience, or some other purpose to be specified by you)

5. Which of your different experiences have in your valuation proved most useful for your present career? (If more than one, rank them)
   a. Education
   b. Training (other than in school)
   c. Travel
   d. Experience
   e. Other (specify)

6. How did you get the idea of establishing (or acquiring or entering) your present business (or, if you are a salaried executive or merely a shareholder, of taking over entrepreneurial responsibility)? (If more than one, rank them)
   a. Through education
   b. Through training (and experience)
   c. Through travelling
   d. Through contacts with other businessmen
   e. Through the influence of a close relative
   f. Through accident (being born into the business, or inheriting it)
   g. Through own interest or initiative or inventiveness
   h. Other (specify)
7. Where did you acquire most of your business experience?
   a. In Lebanon (and/or Syria)
   b. In another country (specify)
8. Were the goods or services which your business produces or offers produced or offered in Lebanon before you started business? Yes. No. Some yes and some no. (Remarks:)
9. On what did you base your decision to introduce into Lebanon the goods or services, or the special processes, characterizing your Establishment — given the element of risk involved in such an introduction? (Check one or more)
   a. Acquaintance with conditions in other countries
   b. Acquaintance, through trade, with the goods you now produce — which encouraged you to shift from importation to production
   c. Encouragement received from foreign technicians consulted
   d. Change in circumstances in Lebanon making such business promising
   e. Mere adventurousness on your part
   f. Availability of resources, and acquaintance with processes, required
   g. Suitability of the goods or services to conditions of the Lebanese economy
   h. Other (specify)
10. Was there encouragement, objection, or indifference from your close social group to your choice of business career? Encouragement Objection Indifference (Remarks:)
11. If there was objection, on what grounds was it based?
12. In your opinion, if you were to start the same career today, would you meet with the same objection from your close social group? Yes. No.

C. *Mobility of Entrepreneurs*

1. Were you in another business career(s) before the present one? Yes. No.
2. If yes, what was it (or what were they)?
3. If yes, what made you change (i.e., discontinue your old activity or add to it)? (Check one or more)
   a. Greater profit in present career
   b. More social prestige
   c. More power
   d. Greater security (more "future")
   e. Better acquaintance with new field of activity
   f. Other (specify)

4. Do you plan to make another shift (or a new one, if you have made none yet)? Yes. No. It depends.
5. If no, why? (Check one or more)
   a. Satisfaction with present activity while wishing to improve it
   b. Desire not to change
   c. Belief that other businesses do not have as good a future or as much security
   d. Inability to handle other business
   e. Inability to raise any necessary additional capital
   f. Other reasons (specify)
6. If yes, do you plan to leave present business altogether? Yes. No.
7. If yes, into what other field of activity do you intend to go? (Specify)
   a. Agriculture
   b. Industry
   c. Construction and real estate
   d. Trade
   e. Finance
   f. Transport
   g. Other services
   h. Other (specify)
8. If yes, are you waiting first for the satisfaction of one or more conditions? (Check one or more)
   a. Obtaining a special type of knowledge or experience
   b. Finding the necessary capital
   c. Waiting for the market to develop for the goods or services of the new business
   d. Waiting for certain ancillary industries or services to emerge first
   e. Waiting for appropriate changes in the tariff and taxation systems
   f. Waiting for the necessary labour skills to develop
   g. Waiting for a more appropriate political climate
   h. Other (specify)
9. Do you believe it advisable for businessmen in Lebanon to invite participation of non-Lebanese entrepreneurs who have new entrepreneurial ideas? Yes. No. (Remarks:)
10. Would you personally invite such participation in case you felt you needed to supplement your own ideas in an area of enterprise with which you are not fully familiar? Yes. No.
11. What would your attitude be if these entrepreneurs were non-Lebanese Arabs or non-Arabs?
    a. Same attitude
    b. Preference for non-Lebanese Arabs
    c. Preference for non-Arabs
12. Under what conditions, if any, would you be in favour of the government facilitating the entry of non-Lebanese entrepreneurs?

IV. TYPES AND QUALITIES OF ENTREPRENEURS

1. Why did you choose your present career? (Check one or more)
   a. Natural inclination
   b. Urging by elders
   c. To contradict such urging
   d. To follow up father's business career
   e. To avoid father's business career

f. Pecuniary profit considerations
g. Prestige
h. Other (specify)

2. If you were to choose afresh a new career, would you go into the one you now have? Yes. No.
3. If no, what other career would you choose?
4. As you know, different lines of business involve different intensities in capital investment, different rates of turnover, different periods of waiting before returns begin to flow in, and different degrees of rigidity of investment. With this in mind, indicate your preference(s) among the following situations.

a. Undertakings involving heavy investment and considerable waiting before returns begin to flow in, but promising a long period of flow
b. Undertakings involving relatively little investment, a short time to establish, and a quick capital turnover
c. A small profit margin per unit on a large volume of business
d. A large profit margin per unit on a small volume of business
e. Other (specify)

5. In taking major decisions, do you mainly:

a. Make up your mind independently and without consultation with friends or subordinates whose opinion you are not required to take?
b. Consult friends (including close relatives) but not subordinates?
c. Consult subordinates but not outsiders?
d. Consult both subordinates and friends?
e. Consult experts outside the Establishment?
f. Other (specify)

6. In taking a major decision, do you

a. Base yourself more on thorough calculation and statistical evidence?
b. Rely more on your perception and your "feel" of a situation?

7. Do you

a. Have a double entry (debit and credit) system of bookkeeping? Yes. No.
b. Use cost accounting? Yes. No.
c. Engage the services of certified external auditors? Yes. No.
d. Use budgeting and financial planning? Yes. No.
e. Use any or all of the above because you believe in the value of these professional processes, even if there were no legal obligations on you to use them? Yes. No.

8. Do you think that research institutions (economic, engineering, agricultural, etc.) render a valuable service to business? Yes. No.
9. If yes, will you be ready to support them by asking them to make studies for you at a fee? Yes. No.
10. Do you carry personal insurance? Yes. No.
11. Is the Establishment insured at all? Yes. No.
12. If yes, indicate the types of insurance carried for Establishment

V. THE ENTREPRENEUR AND HIS ENVIRONMENT

A. *The Economic Factor*

1. How would your Establishment be affected by the readiness of the market for a new product that is a substitute for the one you produce or trade in, and one that is seemingly a more promising product?

a. Shift as soon as possible to the new product regardless of the risk involved
b. Wait until the new product proves its profitability before making a decision

c. Undersell competitors, or otherwise weaken the prospects of the new product
d. Take some other attitude (specify)

2. How will your business be affected by the introduction of a new process (or machine) that is technically superior to the one you use now?
   a. Will you shift as soon as possible to the new process?
   b. Will you keep your own process but make up for your higher cost through acceptance of a smaller profit margin?
   c. Will you search for another process that is superior both to your own and to the one in competition with it?
3. Before deciding to shift to the new process, if you do, what calculation do you make? Describe briefly:
4. If normally you are not inclined to make such shifts, what are your reasons? (Check one or more)
   a. Learning new know-how is disagreeable
   b. Shifting involves great loss in existing installations
   c. Shifting involves you in new and costly capital investment
   d. Shifting is not usually economical
   e. You do not like change
   f. Other (specify)
5. How do you conceive of yourself as reacting to a situation of general economic prosperity? (Check one or more)
   a. By increasing the volume of business slightly so as also to obtain a rise in the profit margin per unit
   b. By substantially increasing volume even to the point of reaching a smaller profit margin per unit than before
   c. By keeping the same volume of business, but making a much larger margin of profit per unit
   d. By going into another business but keeping the present one as it is
   e. By expanding the present business (in capital and outfit)
   f. Other (specify)
6. If you were to decide to expand your business, what would your preference be as to the source(s) of finance?
   a. Present partners or shareholders (as the case may be)
   b. New partners or shareholders
   c. Borrowing from banks
   d. Borrowing from others
   e. Own sources of funds (outside Establishment)
7. If you were to decide not to expand, would that be because of:
   a. Lack of capital funds?
   b. Fear that prosperity may be short-lived?
   c. Feeling that you cannot handle a large business without sharing your authority with someone else?
   d. Other reasons (specify)
8. How do you conceive of yourself as reacting to a situation of general depression? (Check one or more)
   a. Contract your business (close down part of the business and dismiss some of the workers)
   b. Try to keep same volume of business even at a much lower price and profit
   c. Try to keep same volume of business even if that meant a loss for some time
   d. Other (specify)
9. If you decided not to contract during the early stages of a crisis or a depression, would that be because:
   a. You will expect an improvement in business conditions?
   b. It is hard for your prestige to contract unless it cannot be helped?

c. It is very costly to lay off employees under present labour laws?
d. Other reasons (specify)

10. Which of these types of uncertainty influence you most in your entrepreneurial decisions? (Rank in order of importance)

a. Uncertainty deriving from political conditions (discontinuity of policy, arbitrary change of policy, nepotism, etc.)
b. Uncertainty deriving from changes in tastes and markets and the inability to tell the future of demand
c. Uncertainty deriving from frequent changes in tariffs or taxes
d. Uncertainty deriving from technical change
e. Uncertainty deriving from changes in the costs of inputs
f. Other (specify)

11. Which of the following possible reactions do you consider a satisfactory protection against uncertainty? (Check one or more)

a. Choosing businesses involving little capital investment and yielding quick profit
b. Choosing businesses not highly specialized in which you are able to make easy shifts between products and processes
c. Choosing businesses producing several products in which diversity provides some sort of insurance
d. Having more than one business interest spread geographically or sectorially
e. Engaging the services of professional consultants to enable you to be on the alert to face technical and market uncertainties
f. Other (specify)

12. Given normal conditions in Lebanon (as in 1955 and 1957) which of the following factors do you consider favourable to the expansion of your business, which unfavourable, and which indifferent? (Mark "F" for favourable, "U" for unfavourable, and "I" for indifferent)

a. Salary and wage level
b. Interest rates
c. Tax system
d. Tax level
e. Tariff rates
f. Labour law
g. Other (specify)

13. Do you think there are enough credit facilities in Lebanon for investment purposes or operational purposes in your field of business? Yes. No.

14. If no, which of these types of credit are most urgently needed?

a. Short-term credit (under one year)
b. Medium-term credit (1 to 5 years)
c. Long-term credit (over 5 years)

B. *The Social and Political Factor*

1. What course in life did your father (or the person responsible for your upbringing) most insistently want you to follow?
2. Why?
3. What are the qualities you most require in your business associates, i.e., your partners or senior staff? (Check one or more)

a. Honesty, even if they are not very shrewd businessmen
b. Shrewdness, even if they are not very honest (provided, of course, your own business was not the victim of their attitude to honesty)
c. Hard work
d. Ability to get along well with people (that is, being good public-relations men)
e. Influence in government circles

f. Technical efficiency in your line of business
g. Being a close relative of yours
h. Not being a close relative
i. Willingness to take orders or suggestions readily
j. Independence and ability to operate without your orders or guidance
k. Other (specify)

4. What specific action do you think the government ought to take which would be of benefit to your business? (Indicate one or more)

a. Issue laws to regulate and organize your field of business so that potential competition may be reduced
b. Invest in social overhead capital and public services likely to benefit your business
c. Raise custom tariffs on competitive goods
d. Reduce custom tariffs on raw materials and equipment needed by your business
e. Control labor organizations in order to restrict their power to obtain higher wages
f. Lower taxes
g. Help you export through trade agreements, fairs, marketing facilities, subsidies
h. Treat all businessmen without differentiation and favouritism and apply laws rigourously
i. Base all legislation and policy on more study
j. Consult the business community regularly and seriously prior to business legislation
k. Other (specify)

5. Do you think it advisable or useful for a businessman to devote some of his time and efforts to politics, given Lebanese conditions? Yes. No.
6. If yes, what form should such participation in politics take?
7. Do you associate closely with other businessmen who have the same interest in pressing government to follow (or parliament to legislate) certain policies appropriate to your business? Yes. No.
8. Do you think that a greater degree of central planning involving more government control of economic affairs would:

a. Help businessmen in Lebanon?
b. Harm businessmen in Lebanon?
c. Promote development generally?
d. Retard development generally?
e. Other (specify)

9. What are your suggestions for raising the level of technical knowledge in your field? (Check one or more)

a. Technical training and research in government institutions
b. Technical training and research in private educational institutions
c. Technical training and research in institutions established for the purpose by the business community
d. Sending students and other trainees abroad for training
e. Bringing foreign scientists and technicians for training nationals on the job
f. Other (specify)

10. Given equality of training and readiness to work for about the same salary, whom would you choose to work for you if you needed only one technician?

a. A non-Arab technician
b. An Arab non-Lebanese technician
c. A Lebanese technician

11. Why would you make such a choice?
12. Do you feel there is a shortage of able managers in your field of business in the country? Yes. No. Don't know.
13. If yes, what would you recommend to meet the shortage?

a. Training of managers on the job
b. Training them in technical and educational institutions
c. Hiring foreign managers
d. Other (specify)

14. Do you think there are enough able foremen or supervisors to communicate between management and labour (i.e., to play the role of business sergeant-majors between the officer class and the rank and file)? Yes. No. Don't know.

15. Do you believe the presence of foremen or supervisors

a. Necessary for efficient operation?
b. Unnecessary because their function is not significant?
c. Necessary, but their function of communication of orders, establishing discipline, and supervising work can be performed by you or the manager?
d. Depends on the size of business?

16. Do you think there are under present conditions enough technicians and skilled workers in the country for your type of business? Yes. No. Don't know.

17. Do you provide for the training of personnel in your organization apart from the training they acquire on the job? Yes. No.

18. What is your favourite policy with regard to other establishments producing (or offering) the same products (or services) as yours and likely to be a business threat to yours or close substitutes of yours? (Check one or more)

a. Coming to terms with them regarding operations
b. Just ignoring them in the belief that there is room for you both
c. Trying to force them out of the market by buying them out
d. Trying to force them out of the market by underselling them
e. Trying to force them out by developing better distribution services
f. Trying to force them out by improving quality and service
g. Trying to force them out by reducing own costs
h. Other (specify)

19. What, in your opinion, will lead to faster development in the country?

a. A mainly competitive structure of business (involving numerous establishments, with none very large, in every field of business)
b. A mainly monopolistic structure or one of restricted competition (involving a relatively small number of establishments, in every field of business)
c. A mainly government-operated structure

20. Are you in favour of concessions of a monopolistic nature granted by the government to individual businessmen or corporations to develop large projects of a public utility nature? Yes. No.

VI. THE MOTIVES OF THE ENTREPRENEUR

1. It has been stated that the entrepreneur is the factor that gets the most handsome reward or the most ruthless punishment in the enterprise system, depending on whether he succeeds or fails in business. True? False?

2. Which, in your opinion, are the *three* most powerful motives in business (listed in their order of importance) in the following list?

a. Pecuniary profit
b. Power

c. Prestige and status
d. Sense of achievement
e. Satisfaction in expansion in one's business
f. Philanthropy and social service through one's money
g. Other (specify)

3. What is the minimum range of net profit rates per annum you consider adequate for your investment? to per cent.
4. Would you move your investment out if your profit dropped below the lower end of that range? Yes. No.
5. If no, at what lower rate would you consider the necessity of moving out? per cent.
6. What are the factors you would consider before withdrawing (if you decide to withdraw) your investment from the Establishment in case that lower rate of profit persisted?
7. What do you consider the surplus remaining after the deduction of total costs from total revenue?

a. Profit
b. Salary
c. Interest

8. Do you believe it advisable for an Establishment to have as head a man who does not own a part of its capital? Yes. No.
9. What determines your choice of size and capacity of the business? (Check one or more)

a. Efficiency of size chosen
b. Availability of capital
c. Size of market
d. Availability of raw materials (inputs)
e. Availability of skilled labour and personnel
f. Nature of product
g. Your ability to cope with the size chosen
h. Other (specify)

10. Have there been large changes in the size of the Establishment since you assumed responsibility in it? Yes. No.
11. If yes, were these changes ones of:

a. Expansion?
b. Contraction?

12. In trying to promote your sales, do you mainly:

a. Catch up with changes already occurring in consumers' tastes by studying market conditions and following the whims of the market?
b. Influence tastes by advertising, demonstration, distribution of free samples, etc.?

VII. REJUVENATION OF THE ENTREPRENEURIAL SPIRIT

1. Do you usually visit fairs where technical advances are exhibited? Yes. No.
2. Do you subscribe to technical journals or buy technical books (for yourself or your staff) to keep up with such advances? Yes. No.
3. Have you ever tried, or do you plan, to evolve new methods or processes inside your business? Yes. No.

VIII. MANIFESTATIONS OF SUCCESS IN ENTREPRENEUR'S OPINION

1. In your opinion, what manifestations constitute entrepreneurial success? (Check four or less)
   a. Large profits
   b. A certain type or size of wealth
   c. Expansion in the business one operates
   d. Branching off into other fields of activity
   e. Assurance of continuity in the business
   f. Increase in product variety
   g. Introduction of important technical improvements
   h. Change of form of business organization (from partnership to corporation, for example)
   i. Improving product quality, without expansion in size of business
   j. Helping entrepreneurial talent emerge, that is, seeing ex-employees or associates emerge as entrepreneurs on their own (thanks to training or experience gained in your business)
   k. Other (specify)
2. Do you plan to retire from business at some future date? Yes. No.
3. If yes, at what age?
4. What do you intend to do after retirement?
5. Have you already any plans for the handing over in due course of your functions and responsibility? Yes. No.
6. What would you rather your son (or heir) did, even if he is already established?
   a. Continue with the business you are in
   b. Move into another business
   c. Leave business altogether
   d. Take up a profession
   e. Go into government or politics
   f. Emigrate from Lebanon
   g. Other (specify)
7. Do you hold (or have you held) any unpaid position of significance in the field of social service? Yes. No.
8. What are the most notorious failings in others which you try to avoid? (Check four or less)
   a. Ostentation in spending
   b. Ostentation in investment
   c. Participation in politics
   d. Aloofness from politics
   e. Long holidays
   f. Short (or even no) holidays
   g. Quick expansion of business
   h. Contraction of business
   i. Stagnation at same size of business
   j. Branching off into other fields of business
   k. Concentration on one field of business
   l. Career inconsistency
   m. Lack of planning
   n. Other (specify)

APPENDIX C

Complete List of 472 Tables Based on the Questionnaires

NOTE: These tables, based on the completed questionnaires of the 207 entrepreneurs, are reproduced on Microfilm No. 61-1696, Photographic Department, Widener Library, Harvard University. Facsimiles of particular tables may be ordered by mail. Complete facsimiles are on deposit in the Harvard College Library, the Library of Congress, and the library of the American University of Beirut.

In the following list, the titles are given in brief form for convenience. The first 133 tables are straight tabulations, each describing the business leaders with respect to a particular variable, such as age, religion, source of capital, occupation of father, or plans for retirement. The rest of the tables are cross-tabulations, each associating one variable with another — for example, age with reactions to new products, or schooling with the use of double-entry bookkeeping. These cross-tabulations are grouped according to the following independent variables: Age (Tables 134–229); Marital status (230–239); Children (240–250); Religion (251–279); Schooling (280–325); Economic sector (326–418); Participation in other establishments (419); and Form of ownership (420–472).

STRAIGHT TABULATIONS (1–133)

Total number and percentage distribution of:

1. Entrepreneurs by sector
2. Entrepreneurs by position in establishment
3. Entrepreneurs by age group
4. Entrepreneurs by marital status
5. Married or formerly married entrepreneurs by children
6. Establishments by fields of activity

7. Entrepreneurs by participation in other establishments
8. Entrepreneurs by nature of participation
9. Entrepreneurs by number of establishments in which they participate
10. Establishments by form of ownership
11. Entrepreneurs by years of schooling
12. Entrepreneurs by level of education
13. Entrepreneurs by father's original nationality
14. Entrepreneurs by pre-entrepreneurial travel
15. Entrepreneurs by purpose of travel
16. Entrepreneurs by religion
17. Entrepreneurs by place of birth
18. Establishments by age
19. Entrepreneurs by years of work in present position
20. Establishments by occurrence of change in ownership
21. Establishments by peak number of employees
22. Establishments by sources of capital
23. Entrepreneurs who provided capital from their family resources, by source of capital
24. Establishments with capital from another business, by sector
25. Entrepreneurs with capital from family resources, by source
26. Most important entrepreneurial functions by rank
27. Establishments by delegation of entrepreneurial authority
28. Entrepreneurs by persons sharing authority with them
29. Powers of persons sharing authority, by type of power
30. Establishments by existence of administrative divisions
31. Establishments by type of administrative divisions
32. Establishments by the existence of branches
33. Entrepreneurs by present nationality
34. Non-Lebanese entrepreneurs by country of origin
35. Non-Lebanese entrepreneurs by date of immigration
36. Non-Lebanese entrepreneurs by circumstances of emigration
37. Non-Lebanese entrepreneurs by reasons for choosing Lebanon for residence

38. Father's occupation or business by type
39. Entrepreneurs by traditionality of father's occupation or business in the family
40. Entrepreneurs by number of generations father's occupation or business has been in the family
41. Father's important sources of income, by type
42. Entrepreneurs by previous work for other entrepreneurs
43. Entrepreneurs by date they started as entrepreneurs
44. Most valuable experience for career, by rank
45. Manner in which idea of the business obtained, by rank
46. Entrepreneurs by place where experience mostly acquired
47. Establishments by novelty of their goods or services
48. Entrepreneurs by basis of decision to introduce new goods or services
49. Entrepreneurs by attitude of close social group to career
50. Grounds of objection to career, by type of objection
51. Entrepreneurs who met with objection by likelihood of objection today
52. Entrepreneurs by experience in a previous business career
53. Entrepreneurs' previous career by type
54. Entrepreneurs who have shifted career by reason for shift
55. Entrepreneurs by intention to shift to another career
56. Entrepreneurs' reasons for not intending to shift
57. Entrepreneurs who plan to shift by intention with regard to present business
58. Career into which entrepreneurs plan to shift
59. Entrepreneurs by conditions to be satisfied before shift
60. Entrepreneurs by attitude to entry of foreign entrepreneurs
61. Entrepreneurs by attitude to personal association with foreign entrepreneurs
62. Entrepreneurs' attitude to nationality of foreign entrepreneurs
63. Entrepreneurs' conditions for entry of foreign entrepreneurs
64. Entrepreneurs' reasons for choosing present career
65. Entrepreneurs by fresh choice of career

66. Entrepreneurs who would choose other career, by type
67. Entrepreneurs' preference for capital intensity and profit margin
68. Entrepreneurs' attitude to consultation
69. Entrepreneurs by extent of dependence on calculation in decision-making
70. Entrepreneurs by use of double-entry bookkeeping
71. Entrepreneurs by use of cost accounting
72. Entrepreneurs by use of external audit
73. Entrepreneurs by use of budgeting and financial planning
74. Entrepreneurs by belief in value of professional services
75. Entrepreneurs by belief in value of research
76. Entrepreneurs by willingness to seek research services
77. Entrepreneurs by personal insurance
78. Establishments by insurance
79. Insured establishments by type of insurance
80. Entrepreneurs by type of reaction to new products
81. Entrepreneurs by type of reaction to new processes
82. Entrepreneurs not inclined to shift to new processes by reasons
83. Entrepreneurs' reactions to general prosperity
84. Entrepreneurs' preference for sources of finance for expansion
85. Entrepreneurs' causes for not expanding in prosperity
86. Entrepreneurs' reactions to depression
87. Entrepreneurs not inclined to contract business in depression, by reasons
88. Most important types of uncertainty for business, by rank
89. Entrepreneurs' reactions to uncertainty, by type
90. Entrepreneurs by factors favorable or unfavorable to expansion of business
91. Entrepreneurs by views on credit facilities
92. Credit most needed by entrepreneurs, by type
93. Entrepreneurs by careers fathers desired for them
94. Qualities most desired by entrepreneurs in their associates
95. Actions entrepreneurs require government to take

96. Entrepreneurs by views on participation in politics
97. Entrepreneurs by preferred form of participation in politics
98. Entrepreneurs by association with other businessmen
99. Entrepreneurs by views on central planning
100. Entrepreneurs by suggestion for raising technical knowledge
101. Entrepreneurs by preference of technician on grounds of nationality
102. Entrepreneurs by reasons for preference
103. Entrepreneurs by views on the supply of able managers
104. Entrepreneurs by recommendation to increase supply
105. Entrepreneurs by views on supply of able foremen
106. Entrepreneurs by views on foremen for efficient operation
107. Entrepreneurs by views on supply of skilled workers
108. Entrepreneurs by provision of training for personnel
109. Entrepreneurs by policy toward competitors
110. Entrepreneurs by views on economic structure
111. Entrepreneurs by views on concessions for public utilities
112. Entrepreneurs by views on entrepreneurial reward
113. Most important motives in business, by rank
114. Entrepreneurs by minimum range of net profit considered adequate
115. Entrepreneurs by attitude in case profit drops below range
116. Entrepreneurs by rate at which they would move out
117. Entrepreneurs by views on surplus of revenues over costs
118. Entrepreneurs by opinion on heads of establishments who own no capital
119. Entrepreneurs by factors determining size of business
120. Entrepreneurs by changes in size of establishment
121. Establishments which have changed by nature of change
122. Entrepreneurs by method of promoting sales
123. Entrepreneurs by visits to fairs
124. Entrepreneurs by acquisition of business literature
125. Entrepreneurs by attempt to develop new processes
126. Entrepreneurs by views on manifestations of success
127. Entrepreneurs by plans for retirement

128. Entrepreneurs by age at which they plan to retire
129. Entrepreneurs by activity on retirement
130. Entrepreneurs by plans to hand over responsibility
131. Entrepreneurs by careers desired for sons or heirs
132. Entrepreneurs by unpaid activity in social service
133. Entrepreneurs by failings in others which they wish to avoid

Age (134–229)

Cross-tabulation of Age of Entrepreneurs *with:*

134. Sector
135. Participation in other establishments
136. Number of establishments participated in
137. Form of ownership of establishment
138. Years of schooling
139. Level of education
140. Duration of pre-entrepreneurial travel
141. Ways capital of establishment was raised
142. Sources of capital from entrepreneurs' family resources
143. Sector in which capital originated if from other business
144. First choice of entrepreneurial function
145. Second choice of entrepreneurial function
146. Third choice of entrepreneurial function
147. Fourth choice of entrepreneurial function
148. Delegation of entrepreneurial authority
149. Father's occupation or business
150. Previous work for another entrepreneur
151. Date of starting any business as entrepreneur
152. Date of starting present business
153. First choice of most valuable experience for career
154. Second choice of most valuable experience for career
155. Third choice of most valuable experience for career
156. First choice of manner in which idea of business obtained
157. Second choice of manner in which idea of business obtained
158. Third choice of manner in which idea of business obtained

Cross-tabulation of Age of Entrepreneurs *with:*

159. Fourth choice of manner in which idea of business obtained
160. Attitude of close social group to career chosen
161. Grounds for objection to career by close social group
162. Existence of previous business career
163. Entrepreneurs' type of previous career
164. Reasons for changing previous career
165. Plans for shift in career
166. Reasons for not wanting to make a shift in career
167. Intentions with regard to present business upon shifting
168. Intentions with regard to future career upon shifting
169. Conditions to be satisfied before shift is made
170. Views on entry of foreign entrepreneurs
171. Willingness to associate with foreign entrepreneurs
172. Attitude to nationality of foreign entrepreneurs
173. Conditions for entry of foreign entrepreneurs
174. Reasons for choosing present career
175. Fresh choice of career if that were possible
176. Other careers that would be chosen
177. Preference for capital intensity and profit margin
178. Attitude to consultation
179. Extent of dependence on calculation in decision-making
180. Use of double-entry bookkeeping
181. Use of cost accounting
182. Use of external audit
183. Belief in value of research
184. Personal insurance
185. Insurance for establishment
186. Reactions to new products
187. Reactions to new processes
188. Reasons for not being inclined to shift to new processes
189. Reactions to general prosperity
190. Reasons for not favoring expansion in general prosperity
191. Reactions to business depression
192. Reasons for not favoring contraction in depression

Cross-tabulation of Age of Entrepreneurs *with:*

193. First choice of most important type of uncertainty
194. Second choice of most important type of uncertainty
195. Third choice of most important type of uncertainty
196. Fourth choice of most important type of uncertainty
197. Reactions to uncertainty
198. Careers fathers desired for entrepreneurs
199. Qualities most desired by entrepreneurs in their associates
200. Actions entrepreneurs require government to take
201. Views on participation in politics
202. Preference for form of participation in politics
203. Association with other businessmen
204. Views on central planning
205. Suggestions for raising level of technical knowledge
206. Preference of technician on grounds of nationality
207. Reasons for preference of non-Arab technician
208. Reasons for preference of Arab non-Lebanese technician
209. Reasons for preference of Lebanese technician
210. Views on foremen for efficient operation
211. Provision of training for personnel
212. Policy toward competitors
213. Views on economic structure
214. Views on concessions for public utilities
215. First choice of most important motive in business
216. Second choice of most important motive in business
217. Third choice of most important motive in business
218. Minimum range of net profit considered adequate
219. Attitude in case profit drops below range
220. Rate at which entrepreneurs would move out
221. Opinion on heads of establishments who own no capital
222. Method of promoting sales
223. Visits to fairs
224. Acquisition of business literature
225. Manifestations of success in entrepreneurs' view

Cross-tabulation of Age of Entrepreneurs *with:*

226. Plans for retirement
227. Careers desired by entrepreneurs for sons or heirs
228. Unpaid social activity
229. Failings in others which entrepreneurs wish to avoid

Marital Status (230–239)

Cross-tabulation of Marital Status of Entrepreneurs *with:*

230. Existence of previous business career
231. Reasons for changing career
232. Intention to shift to another career
233. Personal insurance
234. First choice of most important motive in business
235. Second choice of most important motive in business
236. Third choice of most important motive in business
237. Plans for retirement
238. Plans to hand over responsibility
239. Unpaid social service

Children (240–250)

Cross-tabulation of Presence of Children *with:*

240. Existence of previous business career
241. Reasons for changing career
242. Intention to shift to another career
243. Personal insurance
244. First choice of most important motive in business
245. Second choice of most important motive in business
246. Third choice of most important motive in business
247. Plans for retirement
248. Plans to hand over responsibility
249. Careers desired by entrepreneurs for sons or heirs
250. Unpaid social service

Religion (251–279)

Cross-tabulation of the Religion of Entrepreneurs *with:*

251. Date of founding of business
252. Attitude of close social group to career
253. Existence of previous business career
254. Previous career by type
255. Reasons for changing previous career
256. Existence of plans for shift in career
257. Intentions with regard to present business upon shifting
258. Intentions with regard to future career upon shifting
259. Views on entry of foreign entrepreneurs
260. Attitude to nationality of foreign entrepreneurs
261. Attitude to consultation
262. Extent of dependence on calculation in decision-making
263. Personal insurance
264. Careers fathers desired for entrepreneurs
265. Qualities most desired by entrepreneurs in their associates
266. Views on participation in politics
267. Views on central planning
268. Preference of technician on grounds of nationality
269. Policy toward competitors
270. Views on economic structure
271. Views on concessions for public utilities
272. First choice of most important motive in business
273. Second choice of most important motive in business
274. Third choice of most important motive in business
275. Views on surplus of revenues over costs
276. Manifestations of success in entrepreneurs' view
277. Careers desired by entrepreneurs for sons or heirs
278. Unpaid social service
279. Failings in others which entrepreneurs wish to avoid

Schooling (280–325)

Cross-tabulation of Schooling of Entrepreneurs *with:*

280. Religion
281. First choice of entrepreneurial function
282. Second choice of entrepreneurial function
283. Third choice of entrepreneurial function
284. Fourth choice of entrepreneurial function
285. Willingness to delegate authority
286. Existence of administrative divisions
287. Present nationality of entrepreneurs
288. Father's occupation or business
289. Date of starting any business as entrepreneur
290. Date of starting present business
291. First choice of most valuable experience for career
292. Second choice of most valuable experience for career
293. Third choice of most valuable experience for career
294. First choice of manner in which idea of business obtained
295. Second choice of manner in which idea of business obtained
296. Third choice of manner in which idea of business obtained
297. Fourth choice of manner in which idea of business obtained
298. Views on entry of foreign entrepreneurs
299. Preference for capital intensity and profit margin
300. Attitude to consultation
301. Extent of dependence on calculation in decision-making
302. Use of double-entry bookkeeping
303. Use of cost accounting
304. Use of external audit
305. Belief in value of research
306. Qualities most desired by entrepreneurs in their associates
307. Actions entrepreneurs desire government to take
308. Views on participation in politics
309. Views on central planning
310. Suggestion for raising level of technical knowledge

Cross-tabulation of Schooling of Entrepreneurs *with:*

311. Preference of technician on grounds of nationality
312. Recommendations to increase supply of able managers
313. Views on foremen for efficient operation
314. Views on economic structure
315. Views on concessions for public utilities
316. First choice of most important motive in business
317. Second choice of most important motive in business
318. Third choice of most important motive in business
319. Views on surplus of revenues over costs
320. Views on heads of establishments who own no capital
321. Visits to fairs
322. Acquisition of business literature
323. Manifestations of success in entrepreneurs' view
324. Plans for retirement
325. Failings in others which entrepreneurs wish to avoid

SECTOR (326–418)

Cross-tabulation of Sector of Establishment *with:*

326. Fields of activity
327. Form of ownership
328. Years of schooling of entrepreneurs
329. Level of schooling of entrepreneurs
330. Original nationality of entrepreneurs' fathers
331. Pre-entrepreneurial travel
332. Entrepreneurs' religion
333. Years of work in present position by entrepreneurs
334. Peak number of employees
335. Ways capital of establishment was raised
336. Sector in which capital originated if from other business
337. Sources of capital from entrepreneurs' family resources
338. First choice of entrepreneurial function
339. Second choice of entrepreneurial function
340. Third choice of entrepreneurial function

Cross-tabulation of Sector of Establishment *with:*

341. Fourth choice of entrepreneurial function
342. Entrepreneurs' willingness to delegate authority
343. Existence of administrative divisions
344. Existence of branches
345. Enterpreneurs' present nationality
346. Occupation or business of entrepreneurs' fathers
347. Traditionality of father's occupation or business in family
348. Previous work for another entrepreneur by entrepreneurs
349. Date of starting any business by entrepreneurs
350. Date of starting present business by entrepreneurs
351. First choice of most valuable experience for career
352. Second choice of most valuable experience for career
353. Third choice of most valuable experience for career
354. First choice of manner in which idea of business obtained
355. Second choice of manner in which idea of business obtained
356. Third choice of manner in which idea of business obtained
357. Fourth choice of manner in which idea of business obtained
358. Novelty of goods or services of establishments
359. Basis of decision to introduce new goods or services
360. Attitude of social group to career chosen by entrepreneurs
361. Grounds for objection to career by close social group
362. Existence of previous business career for entrepreneurs
363. Entrepreneurs' type of previous career
364. Entrepreneurs' reasons for changing previous career
365. Entrepreneurs' views on entry of foreign entrepreneurs
366. Conditions for entry of foreign entrepreneurs
367. Entrepreneurs' reasons for choosing present career
368. Entrepreneurs' preference for capital intensity and profit margin
369. Entrepreneurs' attitude to consultation
370. Extent of dependence by entrepreneurs on calculation in decision-making
371. Use of double-entry bookkeeping
372. Use of cost accounting

Cross-tabulation of Sector of Establishment *with:*

373. Use of external audit
374. Use of budgeting and financial planning
375. Belief by entrepreneurs in value of research
376. Personal insurance for entrepreneurs
377. Insurance for establishment
378. Entrepreneurs' reactions to new products
379. Entrepreneurs' reactions to new processes
380. Entrepreneurs' reactions to general prosperity
381. Entrepreneurs' preference for sources of finance for expansion
382. Entrepreneurs' reactions to business depression
383. First choice of most important type of uncertainty
384. Second choice of most important type of uncertainty
385. Third choice of most important type of uncertainty
386. Fourth choice of most important type of uncertainty
387. Entrepreneurs' reactions to uncertainty
388. Entrepreneurs' views on salary and wage level
389. Entrepreneurs' views on level of interest rates
390. Entrepreneurs' views on tax system
391. Entrepreneurs' views on tax level
392. Entrepreneurs' views on level of tariff rates
393. Entrepreneurs' views on labor law
394. Entrepreneurs' views on credit facilities
395. Entrepreneurs' views on types of credit most needed
396. Qualities most desired by entrepreneurs in their associates
397. Actions entrepreneurs require government to take
398. Entrepreneurs' views on central planning
399. Entrepreneurs' views on supply of able managers
400. Entrepreneurs' recommendations to increase supply
401. Entrepreneurs' views on supply of able foremen
402. Entrepreneurs' views on foremen for efficient operation
403. Entrepreneurs' views on supply of skilled workers
404. Provision of training for personnel
405. Policy toward competitors
406. Entrepreneurs' views on economic structure

Cross-tabulation of Sector of Establishment *with:*

407. First choice of most important motive in business
408. Second choice of most important motive in business
409. Third choice of most important motive in business
410. Entrepreneurs' attitude in case profit drops below range of adequate rates
411. Entrepreneurs' views on surplus of revenues over costs
412. Entrepreneurs' views on factors determining size of business
413. Entrepreneurs' method of promoting sales
414. Entrepreneurs' visits to fairs
415. Acquisition of business literature by entrepreneurs
416. Manifestations of success in enterpreneurs' view
417. Careers desired by entrepreneurs for sons or heirs
418. Failings in others which entrepreneurs wish to avoid

Participation

Cross-tabulation of entrepreneurs' Participation in Other Establishments *with.*

419. Number of establishments participated in

Form of Ownership (420–472)

Cross-tabulation of Form of Ownership of Establishment *with:*

420. Original nationality of entrepreneurs' fathers
421. Entrepreneurs' pre-entrepreneurial travel
422. Date of founding
423. Peak number of employees
424. First choice of entrepreneurial function
425. Second choice of entrepreneurial function
426. Third choice of entrepreneurial function
427. Fourth choice of entrepreneurial function
428. Delegation of entrepreneurial authority
429. Existence of administrative divisions
430. Present nationality of entrepreneurs

Cross-tabulation of Form of Ownership of Establishment *with:*

431. Date of starting any business by entrepreneurs
432. Date of starting present business by entrepreneurs
433. Place where entrepreneurs acquired most experience
434. Plans for shift in career by entrepreneurs
435. Preference for capital intensity and profit margin by entrepreneurs
436. Entrepreneurs' attitude to consultation
437. Extent of dependence on calculation in decision-making
438. Use of double-entry bookkeeping
439. Use of cost accounting
440. Use of external audit
441. Use of budgeting and financial planning
442. Belief in value of research by entrepreneurs
443. Insurance for establishment
444. Entrepreneurs' reactions to new products
445. Entrepreneurs' reactions to new processes
446. Entrepreneurs' reactions to general prosperity
447. Entrepreneurs' preference for sources of finance for expansion
448. Entrepreneurs' reactions to business depression
449. First choice of most important type of uncertainty
450. Second choice of most important type of uncertainty
451. Third choice of most important type of uncertainty
452. Fourth choice of most important type of uncertainty
453. Entrepreneurs' views on salary and wage levels
454. Entrepreneurs' views on level of interest rates
455. Entrepreneurs' views on tax system
456. Entrepreneurs' views on tax level
457. Entrepreneurs' views on tariff rates
458. Entrepreneurs' views on labor law
459. Qualities most desired by entrepreneurs in their associates
460. Provision of training for personnel
461. Policy toward competitors
462. First choice of most important motive in business
463. Second choice of most important motive in business

Cross-tabulation of Form of Ownership of Establishment *with:*

464. Third choice of most important motive in business
465. Entrepreneurs' attitude in case profit drops below range of adequate rates
466. Entrepreneurs' views on surplus of revenues over costs
467. Entrepreneurs' views on heads of establishments who own no capital
468. Entrepreneurs' views on factors determining size of business
469. Manifestations of success in entrepreneurs' view
470. Entrepreneurs' plans for retirement
471. Entrepreneurs' plans to hand over responsibility
472. Careers desired by entrepreneurs for sons or heirs

NOTES

Chapter 1. THE ENVIRONMENT

1. Much of the material in this chapter is based on an earlier essay by the author, "Lebanon: Special Economic Problems Arising from a Special Structure," in *Middle East Economic Papers, 1957* (Economic Research Institute, American University of Beirut), pp. 60–88.

2. The Constitution contains both a guarantee of religious freedom and equality of opportunity, and a stipulation for an equitable representation of the communities in public employment and in the cabinet. For discussion of this and related matters see two books by A. F. Hourani, *Syria and Lebanon* (London: Royal Institute of International Affairs, 1945) and *Minorities in the Arab World* (London: Royal Institute of International Affairs, 1947).

3. For a fuller discussion of this question, see Clyde G. Hess, Jr., and Herbert L. Bodman, Jr., "Confessionalism and Feudality in Lebanese Politics," *Middle East Journal*, Winter 1954, pp. 10–26.

4. Contact with the West is of long standing. As early as the reign of the forceful and open-minded Fakhr ad-Din al Ma'ni in the sixteenth century, trade with Europe was encouraged, at a time when the other Asian and African parts of the Ottoman Empire were largely closed to intercourse with the West. The friendly atmosphere of Lebanon soon attracted missionaries — French, American, and British — who came over for evangelizing and educational purposes. Their influence is tangible in many forms: in the relatively high degree of literacy, in printing presses, and in schools and universities, as much as in the Western outlook and in the assimilation of Western ideas and adoption of Western institutions. This is perhaps more true of Lebanon than of any country in Asia except Israel; however, in Israel's case the aspects of Westernization and the predominance of Western social and political ideas are not the result of the impact of the West on Asia but of the Western origins of many Israelis.

5. The recent upsurge of good intentions and legislation for reform following the assumption of power by the new regime after the political upheaval of 1958 is too close to us in time to allow any fruitful examination of results. It is worth noting that the regime replaced also came into being on the crest of a wave of outcry for reform that culminated in an upheaval in 1952.

6. No real central bank exists. The institution which performs the functions of a central bank is a foreign concessionary company which operates an issue department as well as a commercial banking department that competes with other banks.

7. Albert Badre, "The National Income of Lebanon," *Middle East Economic*

papers, 1956 (Economic Research Institute, American University of Beirut), pp. 33, 34.

8. These last have found support for their attitude in a statement attributed, perhaps apocryphally, to Paul van Zeeland, who was invited by the Lebanese government in 1948 to examine the French-Lebanese currency agreement. Mr. van Zeeland is reputed to have said, "I don't know what makes the economy work, but it seems to do pretty well. I suggest therefore that you leave it alone." (Quoted by A. J. Meyer, "Economic Thought and Its Application and Methodology in the Middle East," *Middle East Economic Papers, 1956*, p. 74.)

9. In addition to remittances by emigrants and the expenditure of international organizations that have been operating in Lebanon for a decade.

10. Even during the protracted revolt of 1958 the pound kept its value with little stabilization effort by the government.

Chapter 2. IN SEARCH OF ENTREPRENEURS

1. When a government takes the initiative in the economic field, it will also be supplying enterprise. If its agents undertake overhead social investment in public works, education, public health, and like fields, they will be acting as entrepreneurs on the whole-economy level — as "social entrepreneurs." If they act in narrower fields, at the industry or firm level, then they will in fact be acting like entrepreneurs in the ordinary sense.

2. The basic, though partial, differentiation was made in an article by James S. Baster, where he applied the term "growth" to areas where "the behavior of the economic variables determining the size of the national product is not seriously affected by social and institutional change during the period considered," and the term "development" to "backward areas where economic improvement takes place with notable concomitant changes in the social structure." See "Recent Literature on the Economic Development of Backward Areas," *Quarterly Journal of Economics*, November 1954, pp. 585–602. The quotation comes from p. 602.

3. This dual use of the term is borrowed from Arthur H. Cole. See *Business Enterprise in its Social Setting* (Cambridge, Mass., 1959), p. 9.

4. Richard Cantillon, *Essai sur la nature du commerce en général*, quoted in "Entrepreneur," *Encyclopaedia of the Social Sciences* (New York, 1931 ed.), vol. V.

5. A case in point is Schumpeter's writing, early in the present century, with respect to the institutionalization of entrepreneurship and the process of destruction incumbent upon entrepreneurial creative acts. This appears in *The Theory of Economic Development*. Later the same ideas were expressed more strongly in *Business Cycles* and in *Capitalism, Socialism, and Democracy*. Another case is Hawley's anticipation of the shift in the identity of the entrepreneur, from the individual to the firm. See Frederick B. Hawley, *Enterprise and the Productive Process* (New York, 1907).

6. Fritz Redlich has discussed this concept in several places, but especially

in *The Molding of American Banking: Men and Ideas* (New York, vol. 1, 1947; vol. 2, 1952); and in "Ideas: Their Migration in Space and Transmittal over Time," *Kyklos,* vol. VI, no. 4 (1953–54), pp. 301–322.

7. See Joseph A. Schumpeter, *The Theory of Economic Development* (Cambridge, Mass., 1934), p. 66.

8. We use the term in the sense in which Frederick H. Harbison has developed the concept, namely, the totality of services and organs in a firm or industry that provide members of the entrepreneurial group or team with the information that enables them to make decisions of major import. Such services and organs include: economic research, industrial relations, advertising, engineering, and other technical research departments. "Entrepreneurial Organization as a Factor in Economic Development," *Quarterly Journal of Economics,* August 1956, pp. 364–379.

9. In several articles in *Explorations in Entrepreneurial History,* and more recently in his book *Business Enterprise in its Social Setting,* Arthur H. Cole has developed his concept of an "entrepreneurial stream" and an "entrepreneurial system." This system encompasses the various entrepreneurial resources operating in a wide range of industries and activities, as well as the institutions, the economic resources, and the cultural forces in the community, in a relationship of interconnection and interaction. The presence of the system can be detected through a number of manifestations such as a willingness to work hard, the expectation and security of rewards, esteem of time, rationalization of business, the weakening of the pressure of tradition and of kinship loyalties in the determination of business decisions, and so on.

10. Joseph A. Schumpeter, *Business Cycles,* 2 vols., (New York, 1939), I, 102.

11. Schumpeter, *The Theory of Economic Development,* chap. IV.

12. This position is generally in line with that of Arthur H. Cole and Fritz Redlich and a few other scholars who have elaborated the concept of adaptive or derivative innovation. In fact, the former may even feel that my definition is too rigorous for his liking. He would rather restrict the definition to strategic decision-making and leave the question of innovation alone. See Cole, *Business Enterprise in its Social Setting,* pp. 13–15.

13. In Schumpeter's view risk-bearing is not an entrepreneurial function. The risk-bearers — capital-owners and creditors — stand to be rewarded or penalized at the end of operations or of an accounting period.

14. However clear this distinction is conceptually, it is hardly operational and was therefore not used in our field investigation. Only insofar as establishments that had been "killed" through major faulty decisions were not on our list of respondents was the distinction made in practice.

15. This is indicated in research done at the Harvard Research Center in Entrepreneurial History, published in *Explorations in Entrepreneurial History,* and in the special issue of that journal entitled *A Symposium on the Aristocrat in Business,* December 1953. For essentially the same conclusions with regard to the Arab Middle East, see S. N. Fisher, ed., *Social Forces*

in the Middle East (Ithaca, N. Y., 1955). With regard to Japan and India, where the same conclusions apply, the literature is quite extensive.

16. See Chapter 3 for a listing of the services included in the study and those excluded from it.

17. Almost every writer on entrepreneurial theory has indulged, even if to a limited extent, in the developing of typologies or at least in the description of certain isolated types. Joseph A. Schumpeter, Arthur H. Cole, Fritz Redlich, Ralph Linton, G. Heberton Evans, Jr., Yale Brozen, Bert F. Hoselitz, Helen R. Wright, and Clarence Danhof are noted for their explicit discussion of the question of entrepreneurial types. I have, speculatively, offered a few thoughts on Arab entrepreneurs in "Toward an Entrepreneurial Theory for the Arab East," *Explorations in Entrepreneurial History,* April 1958, pp. 123–127.

18. Arthur H. Cole, "An Approach to the Study of Entrepreneurship" in Frederic C. Lane, ed., and Jelle C. Riemersma, ass't. ed., *Enterprise and Secular Change, Readings in Economic History* (Homewood, Ill., 1953), pp. 189–191. An excellent treatment of the subject of typology is contained in Fritz Redlich, "Entrepreneurial Typology," *Weltwirtschaftliches Archiv* (Band 82, Heft 2, 1959), pp. 150–168. In his article Dr. Redlich discusses the grounds for classification and groups the large number of possible typologies under four headings: historical, behavioral, sociological, and (what we may call for brevity) "contextual" types—i.e., according to the business and cultural contexts within which business leaders operate.

19. Thomas C. Cochran developed the concept of the general (nonspecialized) entrepreneur and drew attention to his type and the rationale of his existence in the American society. See, for instance, *Railroad Leaders, 1845–1890: The Business Mind in Action* (Cambridge, Mass., 1953).

20. Not excluding the priesthood. Some of the best wines in Lebanon are produced efficiently by two peacefully competing monastic orders. In feudal Europe some of the best-run and most profitable estates were owned and operated by bishops and their priestly subordinates.

21. "Many economists think that they are approaching a dead end in their effort to erect increasingly elaborate theories upon traditional assumptions concerning business behavior and motivation. They believe that economics will be significantly advanced only by introducing more fruitful postulates and testing the resultant hypotheses against empirical data." Howard Bowen in "The Business Enterprise as a Subject for Research" (Social Science Research Council, Pamphlet No. 11, New York, 1955), p. 8. In point of fact similar feeling has sprung from doubts in the minds of many students in this field of economics. Quite often the case against the profit motive has been overstated — mostly because of the erroneous belief that economic theorists do not take into account motives other than pecuniary profit. Such accusation is the price a theorist pays for the oversimplification of his models. To the extent that he does not state his wider convictions explicitly, he is substantially to blame for the misunderstanding that draws the fire of attack by other social scientists.

Chapter 3. DESIGN AND CONDUCT OF THE STUDY

1. A senior assistant in the present study had been senior assistant in the industrial census, and his firsthand information was valuable in the assessment of industrial establishments as innovators.

2. Two men were instructors in the Department of Economics, American University of Beirut (one the holder of a doctorate from a United States university, the other of a B. Litt. from Oxford University). A third had a bachelor's degree and a law degree, as well as five years' experience in statistical work both in the field and the laboratory. Two more were graduate fellows preparing for a master's degree in economics.

3. Invariably the traditional cup of coffee or some other refreshment was offered to us. In half a dozen cases we had to accept a present: biscuits, chocolates, fruits produced by the respondent. One banker overwhelmed us by presenting each of the nine participants with a gold medallion (worth five dollars) which had been struck for distribution to shareholders and dignitaries on the occasion of the tenth anniversary of the bank.

Chapter 4. ENTREPRENEURS OF LEBANON: A SELF-PORTRAIT

1. Other items of personal information than age were sought, such as place of birth, marital status and children, religious affiliation, schooling, and foreign travel. The cross-tabulation of some of these independent variables with a number of dependent variables will be referred to and discussed in this chapter in other contexts.

2. See Question II/A/1 in the questionnaire (Appendix B) for a listing of these aspects of the entrepreneurial function.

3. Questions II/A/2 and III/B/8 and 9 in the questionnaire (Appendix B).

4. Here I partly agree and partly disagree with the definition of the entrepreneur drawn by Heinz Hartmann in "Managers and Entrepreneurs: A Useful Distinction," *Administrative Science Quarterly,* March 1959, pp. 429–451. In Hartmann's view, the entrepreneur is the one who serves as the source of delegated formal authority, or at least the medium through which formal authority at the highest level flows. I agree that the entrepreneur is a source of authority. But his authority need not originate with him; it can be delegated from above. The *substance* of authority is what matters: does it or does it not permit the entrepreneur (in our definition) to make decisions of an innovational nature?

5. The fascinating story of the spread of Lebanese entrepreneurs into most parts of the world has never been written. Unfortunately it does not fit into the present study.

6. For references to the business habitat of the entrepreneur in Lebanon and to the manner in which he conducts business, see: A. J. Meyer, "Entrepreneurship: The Missing Link in the Arab East?" in *Middle East Economic Papers, 1954* (Economic Research Institute, American University of Beirut); Dalton Potter, "The Bazaar Merchant" in Sydney N. Fisher, ed., *Social Forces in the Middle East* (Ithaca, N. Y., 1955); Arthur E. Mills, *Private Enterprise in Lebanon* (Beirut, 1959).

7. Arthur H. Cole speaks about trade as being a starting point for entrepreneurs generally in many countries. *Business Enterprise in its Social Setting,* pp. 114–115.

8. As in the case of the fathers, "industry" is to be taken to mean manufacturing industry proper as well as transformative production in little workshops and craft shops.

9. Reference here is to Arthur H. Cole's well-known classification of types into empirical (rule-of-thumb), rational (informed), and cognitive (sophisticated). It should be added that the differentiation is both one of type of characteristics and of time or stage of development, as he emphasizes.

10. Valuable pioneering work is being done in the field of motivation by a small number of scholars such as Henry A. Murray, David C. McClelland, John W. Atkinson, Russell A. Clark, and Edgar L. Lowell. Everett E. Hagen deserves special credit as an economist who is using the tools of these psychologists in developing a theory of economic growth.

11. At the start of the inquiry on motives I attempted to find out if Lebanese business practitioners disagreed among themselves as much as economic theorists did a century ago, about the nature of the surplus remaining after costs are deducted from returns. To this end the respondents were asked whether they considered this surplus profit, salary, interest, or some combination of these. The question was not specific, and was accordingly expected to be criticized heavily, if only because it did not indicate whether "total costs" included any remuneration for the entrepreneur. Objections there were, but neither serious nor numerous. Only four persons refused altogether to answer. Profit was named 181 times, interest 29 times, and salary 28 times. (Some of the respondents named two, or even all three, since multiple choice was allowed.)

12. Different writers have emphasized different motives. Schumpeter, for instance, was well aware of the presence of motives other than the maximization of monetary profits (or the minimization of monetary losses). His broader outlook can be proved from his reference to such motives as achievement, creation, the founding of a private kingdom, a dynasty, the will to conquer, the impulse to fulfill, the desire to "succeed for success' sake." (See *The Theory of Economic Development,* p. 93.) Generally speaking, the motives that receive most endorsement by writers on the subject are power, prestige, the urge for creation, the sense of accomplishment or achievement, emulation, the desire to be identified with some successful or prominent group, security, and adventure. Some writers, such as Robert Gordon, Chester Barnard, and Moses Abramovitz add the desire to serve others, the desire to avoid failure, and the fear of failure. G. H. Evans talks of security as mainly motivating the managing entrepreneur; adventure, the innovating entrepreneur; and power, the controlling entrepreneur (in "The Entrepreneur and Economic Theory: A Historical and Analytical Approach," *American Economic Review, Papers and Proceedings,* 1949, p. 336).

13. A good idea of the size of such an undertaking can be obtained by referring to what one writer has said in enumerating the factors influencing

the emergence and type of entrepreneurs. He lists: (1) society's mores (such as rationality, religion, values, position of the idea of innovation itself, etc.); (2) social structure; (3) availability of "new men"; (4) pressure on "Fabian" and "Drone" (i.e., hesitant and unenterprising) entrepreneurs to accept innovations; (5) incentives; (6) access to resources; (7) availability of "promotable" people — people ready to enter entrepreneurial ranks; (8) foreigners — minority groups not greatly inhibited by the majority's social and cultural pressures and traditions and therefore freer to innovate; and (9) entrepreneurial security, involving freedom as well as protection — protection here not to mean shelter against competition but against encroachments on law and order. See Yale Brozen, "Determinants of Entrepreneurial Ability," *Social Research*, Autumn 1954, pp. 339–364.

14. The concept "economic organization" is used here to mean the totality of production units, factors of production, markets, business legislation, economic structure and system — in short, all that could legitimately be considered economic environment in a given country.

INDEX

BOOKS FROM

THE CENTER FOR INTERNATIONAL AFFAIRS

PUBLISHED BY HARVARD UNIVERSITY PRESS

The Soviet Bloc, by Zbigniew K. Brzezinski, 1960 (jointly with the Russian Research Center).

Rift and Revolt in Hungary, by Ferenc A. Váli, 1961.

The Economy of Cyprus, by A. J. Meyer, with Simos Vassiliou, 1962.*

Entrepreneurs of Lebanon, by Yusif A. Sayigh, 1962.*

PUBLISHED BY OTHERS

The Necessity for Choice, by Henry A. Kissinger, 1961. Harper & Brothers.

Strategy and Arms Control, by Thomas C. Schelling and Morton H. Halperin, 1961. Twentieth Century Fund.

United States Manufacturing Investment in Brazil, by Lincoln Gordon and Engelbert L. Grommers, 1962. Harvard Business School.

HARVARD MIDDLE EASTERN STUDIES

1. *Desert Enterprise: The Middle East Oil Industry in Its Local Environment,* by David H. Finnie, 1958.
2. *Middle Eastern Capitalism: Nine Essays,* by A. J. Meyer, 1959.
3. *The Idea of the Jewish State,* by Ben Halpern, 1961.
4. *The Agricultural Policy of Muhammad 'Alī in Egypt,* by Helen Anne B. Rivlin, 1961.
5. *Egypt in Search of Political Community,* by Nadav Safran, 1961 (also a Harvard Political Study).
6. *The Economy of Cyprus,* by A. J. Meyer, with Simos Vassiliou, 1962.*
7. *Entrepreneurs of Lebanon,* by Yusif A. Sayigh, 1962.*

* Published jointly by the Center for International Affairs and the Center for Middle Eastern Studies.

Bei Fragen zur Produktsicherheit wenden Sie sich bitte an:
If you have any questions regarding product safety,
please contact:

Walter de Gruyter GmbH
Genthiner Straße 13
10785 Berlin
productsafety@degruyterbrill.com